Floral
Brunch

1) 2 — footed cake stand (c̄ lip)

2) 1 — Arrange 3 sizes of polished oranges — peled sup

3) → Shiny green leaves around edge tucked in among oranges

4) white & yellow mums c̄ cider center-place in among oranges → be sure often dry enough

5) lemon & lime bunches (2-tone) among orange

6) put on table

7) pour in H₂O

Also by Marjorie Reed with Kalia Lulow
Marjorie Reed's Party Book

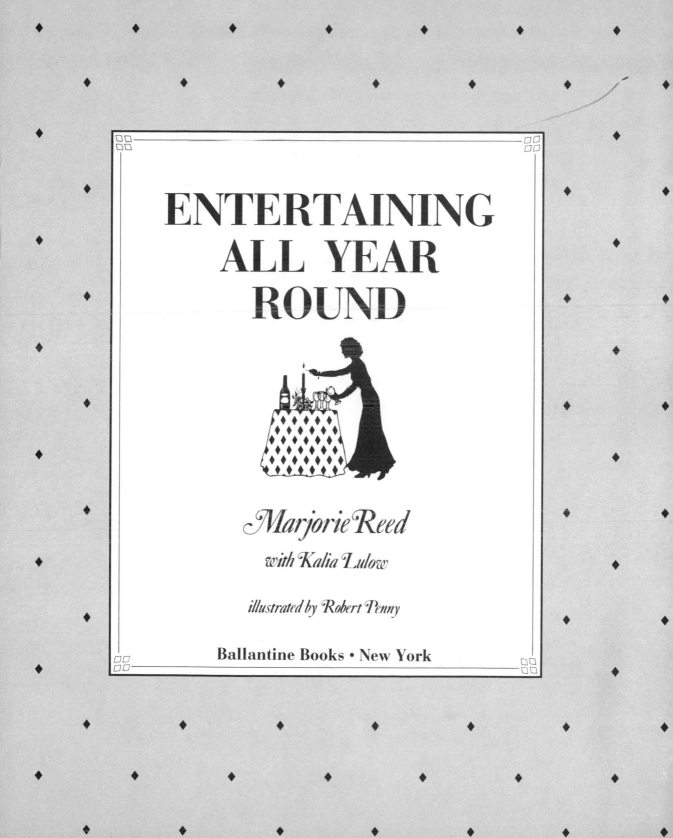

ENTERTAINING ALL YEAR ROUND

Marjorie Reed

with *Kalia Lulow*

illustrated by Robert Penny

Ballantine Books • New York

This book is dedicated to Anne, my mother and my friend.

—Marjorie Reed

ACKNOWLEDGMENTS

We would like to express special thanks to the following people: To Marilyn Kelly our deepest appreciation for her talent and knowledge about food; to Joelle Delbourgo, our editor, our thanks over and over for her undying patience, enthusiasm and wise guidance; and to Robert Penny, the creative illustrator who so deftly transforms ideas and words into images, our affection and thanks.

We'd also like to thank Michelle Russell for her help, and Nancy Burke, without whom this manuscript would never have reached its final, well-typed form. Thanks, too, to the wonderful team who helped put together the color photographs in this book: Jimmy Harris, Alexander White, Beverly Parker, Don Banks, Marilyn Abraham, and Stephen Schmidt. There are others, too. We hope they know who they are.

—Marjorie Reed and Kalia Lulow

Contents

ENTERTAINING ALL YEAR ROUND

Chapter One
THE CALENDAR OF CELEBRATIONS

*Y*ear round the calendar is highlighted by those holidays and special occasions that signal to us: IT'S TIME TO ENTERTAIN!

We look forward to celebrating time-honored traditions: we grow romantic over Valentine's Day, festive on the Fourth of July, downright nostalgic at Christmas. For the eager party giver and the reluctant host alike, these are the special times of the year when we are moved to entertain family and friends.

Special occasions enhance our lives and give us the opportunity to express our feelings for others, to bask in the pleasure of their company. Feelings, flavors, colors, smells—all our sensory experiences are heightened when we celebrate together.

But alas, most of us tend to confine our celebrations to specific holidays marked in red letters on our calendars. Entertaining should not be reserved for certain times of the year, but integrated into our lives. Every day can be a special occasion.

Entertaining All Year Round is a source book for inspiration. It will take you through the calendar year and beyond. For every special occasion, be it Thanksgiving or Easter, your first anniversary or a promotion party for a good friend, you'll find a foolproof party plan. The book has been divided into the four seasons: *winter, spring, summer,* and *fall.* Within each season, there are completed celebrations covering the main holidays of that time of year. In addition, the "Personal Parties" section offers entertainments for those special days such as birthdays, weddings, anniversaries, showers, and events such as moving in or moving up.

The party plans are designed to make entertaining simple and beautiful. From flower arrangements to menus, recipes to table settings, each party is laid out step by important step. Throughout, lovely drawings show you the final results. The luscious color photographs bring you into my home so you can see how I create a festive atmosphere.

The recipes for the special dishes in each party menu are marked with an asterisk indicating that they are located in the cookbook section at the back of the book. This way you can refer to them again and again. Just because your favorite pasta dish appears in a summer party doesn't mean you have to wait till July to use it! You can take ideas for food from any plan and use them to suit yourself.

Each party comes from my heart—it is a reflection of my spirit and taste. I hope that these party plans can help you give parties that are easy and fun *and* reflect your individual spirit. While each occasion has been carefully designed to work as a whole, it is possible to borrow ideas and make your own party plans. The only thing to remember is that all elements of a party must work together. The menu must be suited to the table setting and the serving pieces you use, the decor must work with the overall mood you hope to create—the occasion must be reflected in each aspect. And the colors, textures, and styles of the individual parts of any arrangement must be there for a reason—not because they were just the handiest items! All your parties should be a unified statement of your vision and taste. Then you'll be a confident, comfortable host.

If you take one lesson from this book, I hope it's this: Your life is full of reasons to celebrate! You baked a delicious cake. The harvest moon is full. Your best friend got a promotion. It's Super Bowl Sunday. The new swimming pool is finished. Any one of these events can be a reason to give a party. And if you choose, you can repeat the event next year, too. Before you know it, you'll have a personal calendar full of year-round entertaining traditions. Forging new holidays comes from setting your imagination free. From your dreams come fantasies, and from fantasies come parties that really sparkle.

◇————————————————◇

Chapter Two

THE TEN GOLDEN RULES FOR A GREAT PARTY

*F*rom brunch to buffet, dinner to dancing, any entertainment can be a pleasure to give *and* to attend if you keep the ten golden rules in mind! I have found that these rules unleash the excitement by letting you put aside your worries about basic party organization and dynamics.

There are three areas of concern that we all must contend with whenever we entertain: our hosting techniques, the look of the house, and the food. The golden rules make these potential worries manageable.

HOSTING TECHNIQUES: GETTING YOURSELF PREPARED

RULE ONE: ORGANIZATION IS THE KEY TO EASY ENTERTAINING

* Plan an interesting guest list that includes a variety of people of different occupations, interests, ages.
* Send out invitations at least two weeks ahead of time.
* Plan the theme, mood, or overall look of the party and make sure you have the supplies you need to translate your ideas into reality.
* Write out lists of decorations, food, and cooking requirements. Don't leave anything to chance—because the chance is you'll forget something!

RULE TWO: TAKE TIME FOR YOURSELF—RELAX!

* Schedule last-minute preparations to include time for yourself! You want to feel calm, attractive, and peaceful when you greet your first guest.
* Select clothing that is easy to move in, comfortable, and attractive. The host or hostess can always be slightly more dressed up than the guests.
* Set aside time to run through the party in your head—a mental dress rehearsal—to make sure you have not forgotten anything.

RULE THREE: PERFECT YOUR PARTY DYNAMICS

* Always introduce every guest to the others when they enter.
* "Float" from group to group during the party, checking on conversation, mixing guests, making sure everyone feels included and important.
* Develop a "third eye" that notices overflowing ashtrays, empty glasses, and potential trouble spots.
* Take time to chat, even briefly, with each guest.
* Keep your sense of humor at all times. Once a party begins it has a life of its own, and you can be sure the unpredictable can (and will) happen! Don't let it dampen your spirit.
* Never make small disasters public!! If the appetizer burns, the soufflé falls, or the wine spills, attend to it quickly and quietly.

THE LOOK OF THE HOUSE: SETTING THE PARTY MOOD

RULE FOUR: SPACE EXPANDS WHEN USED CREATIVELY

* No apartment or house is too small for a

party. Use your entire space. Turn the second bathroom into a bar, your bedroom into a buffet area, your kitchen into a self-help serving area. Rearrange furniture. Create indoor picnics if you don't have a dining room. Think creatively!

* Give parties that work with your available space. Throw a cocktail party with guests invited at staggered hours if you must accommodate a large crowd in a small space. Have simple dessert parties if you don't have the facilities to present an entire meal. Just don't let space keep you from enjoying your friends' company!

RULE FIVE: CREATE YOUR OWN PERSONAL STYLE OF PARTY DECORATING

* Have basic props at hand—it cuts time, expense, and eliminates indecision.
* Don't hesitate to use the same touches—with minor changes—over and over. Guests will come to look forward to your way of doing things! You will become distinctive.
* Find your best party format—buffet, sit-down dinner, cocktail party, brunch, whatever suits you. Rely on it.
* Don't ever force a style! If you are naturally formal, so be it. If casual is your spirit, carry it to its beautiful best.

RULE SIX: SPREAD THE PARTY MOOD THROUGHOUT THE HOUSE

* Use lighting and music to set an instant party mood. Candlelight, lamps draped with colored scarves, pink incandescent bulbs, and appropriate background music are the simplest ways to signal "celebrate."
* Put away all personal knickknacks, grooming supplies, etc. The bedroom dresser should be decorated with candles and flowers, not hair spray and yesterday's mail! Put toiletries out of sight in the bathroom.
* Put one decorating touch in the entrance hall or by the front door to make guests feel instantly part of a festive occasion. Flowers, special lighting, or some special arrangement will do the trick.

THE FOOD: COOKING UP A SPLENDID SPREAD WITHOUT EFFORT

RULE SEVEN: YOU DON'T HAVE TO BE A GREAT COOK TO GIVE A GREAT PARTY

* Food, simply prepared and beautifully presented, is always best.
* Don't hesitate to rely on takeout or catered food—if you have tasted it and it meets your standards. Put your efforts into presentation on the platter.
* If cooking is not your strong suit, choose parties that don't call for elaborate food preparation—dessert parties, cocktail parties, or simple teas or brunches.

RULE EIGHT: ALL FOOD SHOULD BE PART OF THE PARTY DECOR

* No plate or platter should ever come to a table "undressed."
* The menu must be compatible with the decor of the party.
* Unusual food presentation can transform the simplest fare into exciting dining. Use hollowed-out vegetables such as cabbage, eggplant, or bell peppers as containers for other food.
* Use serving dishes in new ways for added impact. Old silver creamer and sugar sets can hold sauces; gravy boats can hold breadsticks; wicker baskets can serve as casserole liners. The only limit is your imagination.
* Food should be as beautiful to look at as it is to taste.

RULE NINE: ORGANIZE ALL COOKING AND FOOD SERVICE WELL AHEAD OF TIME

* Write out menus and shopping lists as soon as you begin planning the party. If you want to try new dishes, test them ahead of time. Don't experiment on your guests.
* Plan menus that can be cooked ahead of time, then reheated.
* Rely on cold food to make preparation easy.

* Write out serving schedule. Know when first course, entrée, and dessert will be served. Plan how you will clear and serve each course.
* Keep all food and drinks in separate locations. When having a buffet, don't place drinks on the table with food.
* Don't plan a meal that is too much for one person to handle. If you want to or must, then you will need to have helpers.

THE SPECIAL TOUCH: BRINGING ALL THE RULES TOGETHER

RULE TEN: ALWAYS CREATE AN ELEMENT OF SURPRISE IN EVERY PARTY

* Increase anticipation by always having a surprise element at your parties: one special decorating touch, special food, or a surprise guest (as a matter of fact, you should never reveal your guest list ahead of time!).
* Know that you can't control a party completely—they take on a life of their own once they begin. So tune in to what's happening and go with it; don't fight it or make it fit some preplanned idea you impose.

When you follow these basic guidelines, you'll find you'll have a surprisingly good time at your own parties, and you'll be delighted by the ease with which you can expand your entertaining all year round!

Chapter Three
PLANNING THE PARTY

*T*he key to easy entertaining is a natural, personal style. No matter what the occasion—serving a cup of coffee to a friend or a dinner to the boss—you can express your spirit and taste. We all have a natural style, but it is often hard to translate it into active choices if we don't have self-assurance, or are not well organized.

Style is an elusive, hard-to-define quality—as individual as each of us. But when we look around we see the stylish

people are those who dare to be themselves. So what I've done is translate my own approach to developing an entertaining style into a simple, three-step process: the Party Closet, Creative Party Decorating, and Festive Food Presentation. These techniques can serve as a guide to help you express your own style. They come from my experience of hundreds of parties. I want them to spark your imagination so you can interpret, change, and experiment.

Getting Organized
The first step in planning a party and creating an entertaining style is organization. By putting together your basic party props in a Party Closet you are always prepared and confident that you can arrange the decor beautifully and quickly.

The Party Closet doesn't have to be a

closet. It can be a chest of drawers, a wicker hamper, even a cache of boxes stored in the attic or basement; but whatever area you choose, make it easy to get at. As you develop it, add interesting objects and supplies that you see in shops, tag sales, along the beach—when and wherever a possible party decoration catches your imagination and fancy.

The supplies should form the basis for creating centerpieces, setting the table, preparing food, and handling cleanup.

Creative Party Decorating
Once you have assembled your basic Party Closet, you can expand it to include a few special objects that can be used over and over again in countless ways to create imaginative centerpieces and decorating touches. And, depending on how these items are used, you can create completely different moods and settings.

The basic items in my trademark collection are my favorite ways of expressing my style. A trademark says you know how to make entertaining work for you. Following is a list of items in my collection. Throughout the book you'll see them used in many different party settings. Use them as an inspiration to create your own trademark collection.

Basics

invitations	place mats
name cards	paper napkins
doilies	candles (votives and tapers)
matches	candleholders
paper or plastic plates	vases (various shapes)
coasters	wicker baskets

Possible Props

moss	sequins and glitter
seashells	spray paints
sand	colored cardboard bags and boxes
ribbon and cord	paper party favors (confetti, streamers, fans, etc.)
fabric remnants	clay pots and saucers
tissue paper	

Floral Supplies

floral clay	Styrofoam cubes
oasis	frogs
floral wire	capped bud vials
floral adhesive	branch clippers

Bar Supplies

carafes	bottle openers
decanters	ice tongs and bucket
large glass pitcher	wine/champagne cooler
drink glasses (plastic and glass)	bottle caps or plugs
corkscrews	lemon peeler

Marjorie Reed's Trademark Collection

Glass bowl, 11 inches in diameter, 4¾ quart capacity.

I use this as a vase or to float one single bloom in water over a layer of black rocks or as a container for other centerpiece arrangements. It also works beautifully as a salad bowl or a dish for pasta.

Five bud vases: three are 4 inches high, one is 10 inches high, and one is 13½ inches high.

A single bud can brighten a breakfast tray or bedside table. Grouped together, the vases can form the basis for a delicate but luxurious arrangement. When used in combination with the wooden stands or the tambori tables that are also part of my collection, they become even more versatile.

Three tambori tables: one is 9½ by 11½ by 9½ inches high: one is 7½ by 9 by 9 inches high, and one is 6 by 7 by 7½ inches high.

These tables are absolutely essential. They allow you to bring variety of height and rhythm to table settings, food presentation, and flower arrangements. I use them to hold serving dishes, potted plants, vases, candles, and art objects. You can drape them with fabric or leave them uncovered.

Four bamboo Chinese trays, from 14¼ inches square to 11¾ inches square.

Food looks beautiful when presented on these trays. Pass hors d'oeuvres on them or use them for place mats. They also are a good backdrop for flower arrangements and centerpieces. The bud vases arranged on a tray have an elegant look. Small pots of spring blooms nestled into a moss-filled tray make instant centerpieces.

Three wicker baskets with glass liners, 5 inches high by 2¾ inches wide.

These delicate baskets and liners make a great addition to any table. Whether used to hold dips and sauces, cookies, tea sandwiches or filled with candies, they are as practical as they are pretty. With a mini-bouquet of flowers they become a useful part of a centerpiece. Furthermore, the liners and baskets can be used separately.

Three votive candles and glass holders.

Candlelight is a necessity at any evening party. Votive candles are the best choice because they are subtle and can be used in large numbers to cast a warm glow without being overwhelming. The glass holders are also useful as small serving cups and as mini-vases for single buds in a centerpiece or arrangement.

Three black lacquered wooden stands: two 3½ inches wide by 2½ inches high, one 8¾ inches wide by 5 inches high.

These stands, like the tambori tables, provide instant variety of height and rhythm to any table. You can put candles on them or serving bowls, vases of flowers or art objects.

Decorative items:

- bag of Spanish moss to put on top of plants
- bag of black shiny pebbles to fill the glass bowl
- wire frog to hold flowers

Artful Table Settings

Now you have all the props, you can begin to develop the art of table setting and arranging. Nothing is more important to setting the mood of a party than the look of the table and the house. It's your chance to let your imagination bloom, to unleash your fantasies. This is my favorite aspect of giving a party.

Table settings have a life of their own—a special energy. The basic components are:
> beauty
> simplicity
> style
> impact
> appropriateness.

These qualities are created by an awareness of the rhythm, texture, colors, and height of the components on any table. Just like a painting, a table setting must be artfully composed.

Think of the tabletop as a canvas. The line of the arrangement can stretch across the entire length, be scattered across the tabletop or focused on one corner. To achieve *rhythm* vary the size and placement of objects in an arrangement. *Texture* is created by the combinations of objects with contrasting or similar surfaces: smooth, shiny green leaves, with rough earthy stone, ceramic, or fabric. Any combination should create impact and make a statement. *Color*, like texture, can contrast or harmonize, but it is important that the effects, too, be intentional, planned, well-controlled. *Height* is the final variable on a table, and generally speaking, you will create a more beautiful arrangement when some parts are tall, some mid-range, and some short. Transitions should be smooth and carry the eye from one element to the next. Let's look at some basic arrangements and see how to put this all together. Remember an arrangement must never interfere with conversation at the table.

Festive Food Presentation

The last touch, but not the least, in carrying out your entertaining style is the presentation of the food on the plates with the serving pieces. Food color, texture, and shape are the three components you can work with. Like a vase that holds a flower arrangement, a plate is a frame for food. Its color or design must not hide the food or make it look haphazard. Once you have selected dishes that are the appropriate size, shape, and color for each food served, there are five basic patterns of food arrangement that you can rely on, which are illustrated below.

Each of these basic patterns can be used to create many different looks. From elegant French fare to simple crudités, no item on your menu should be put on a party table without thought to its presentation.

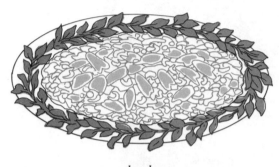

border

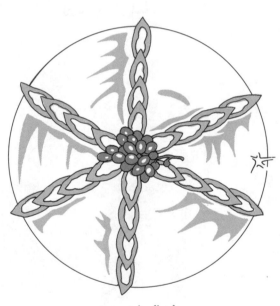

geometric display

circular display

floral display

single focus

Now you're ready to start the calendar of year-round entertainments. Remember these party plans are a source book. Make the ideas fit your individual tastes and needs. Don't hesitate to take decor, menu, and organizational tips from many parties and use them as you want! Let the "recipes" for entertaining serve as a basis for your parties. You can change the garnishes to suit your style.

CALENDAR
PARTIES

Chapter Four
SPRING INTO ACTION

At last, the relief, the joy, the pure pleasure of spring! Gone are the hermit habits of winter. The holidays of this season—from the rites of spring, Easter and Passover, to Mother's and Father's Day—symbolize a rebirth, a reawakening of our senses. We reach out to celebrate the earth's renewal. We feel an expansiveness of spirit that makes this a grand time to spread our wings, and gather our friends around us for the sheer fun of it!

With this blossoming of your spirit comes a special impulse to let loose, to shed your coats and your restraints. The parties of this season may be as casual as a barbecue or as fancy as a tea dance, as cozy as a Mother's Day breakfast or as open as a spring picnic in the grass for your friends and their children. But no matter what format your entertaining takes it should reflect the graceful beauty of the blossoming season.

The Plants of Spring
In winter, we use plants to shield us from the barren outside world. In spring they revive us, infusing us with energy. The simplest budding branch brought indoors sheds a light in any room. The crocus, peering through the last blanket of snow, bold yellow daffodil, delicate pink quince, aromatic hyacinth, or graceful ruffled tulips can transform a room more than any other decorating touch.

So wash off the dull leaves of your houseplants, place pots of flowers around the bases of your indoor trees, make simple window boxes out of tin trays sprayed white or oblong wicker baskets. Let spring in and you have a basic setting for any spring party.

The variety of plants available in the spring can be broken down into four groups: bulbs, branches, cut flowers, and potted plants. You don't need a greenhouse full to brighten up your home. Here are my very favorites; you can try them in the suggested arrangements or experiment with your own preferences. The most important thing to remember is that they can set the stage for entertaining beautifully with minimum effort and maximum effect.

Bulbs	Branches	Cut Flowers	Potted Plants
tulips	quince	anemone	primrose
narcissus	dogwood	African daisies	azalea
daffodil	wisteria	snapdragons	cineraria
iris	lilac	calla lilies	pocketbook plant
	pussy willow		

Tips on Arranging

Bulbs should be set out in low, flat, clear glass or opaque saucers so you can see the bulb itself. Line saucer with a 2 inch layer of flat stones or pebbles. Pour in enough water to just cover the stones. Push bulbs halfway down into stones. *Hints*: blow gently into tulips to get them to open; daffodils last longer if kept in shallow water.

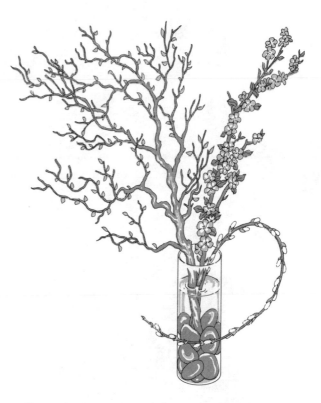

Branches can stand alone magnificently. Don't crowd them in a vase. One or two stalks are all that's needed in any container. Let the line of the branch carry the eye. *Hints*: to keep branches fresh longer, make three 2-to-4-inch lengthwise slashes in the base of the stem. This assures proper water flow. Also, to shape pussy willow branches, soak in warm water and bend in curved shape.

Cut Flowers can be used singly in bud vases, grouped together in a one-color arrangement, or all mixed together in a larger, more dramatic display. *Hint*: warm water makes buds open sooner.

Potted Plants clustered together make an instant garden setting. I love to place them around the bases of the trees in my living room. Or try putting different types and sizes of potted blooms into large wicker baskets, on trays, or in oversized ceramic bowls.

The Trademark Look

Using the trademark wicker basket, 18-inch glass cylinder and 12-inch glass bowl you can create spring arrangements easily.

Don't miss
Gloria and Jerry
and family's

Rite of Spring

Mid-May   *1 P.M.*

Bring the whole family
RSVP

*N*o matter what your religion, early spring is a time for celebration. Easter, Passover, carnival, Holi (in India) are a chance to give thanks for the passing of winter. This basic spring party can be used for any such occasion. If you have a garden or patio, let the party spill over outdoors for a long afternoon of relaxed spring pleasures.

MENU

12–15 People

White Wine

Tea

Fruit Juice Punch

Fresh Dill Cream Cheese Spread

Assorted Crackers and Rolls

*Devilled Eggs with Varied Fillings
(Herbs, Caviar, Smoked Salmon)*

** Sugar Glazed Baked Ham
Smoked Turkey*

** German Potato Salad with Bacon
Dressing*

Cold Green Beans Vinaigrette

Asparagus in Mustard Sauce

Coffee

*Fresh Fruit Compote (Sliced Berries,
Kiwis, Apples, Grapes, Melons)*

* Lemon Bars   Fudgy Brownies

Children's Menu

Herb Filled Devilled Eggs

Ham Sandwiches

Cup of Fresh Fruit

Lemon Bars   Fudgy Brownies

Invitations

A leaf- or flower-shaped invitation on plain pastel paper is the perfect mood setter for this party. You can find them at your local card shop, or if you're feeling inventive, trace a tree leaf on paper and cut it out.

SETTING THE STAGE

The key to this party's look is the combination of unexpected shapes and sizes of terra-cotta pots and containers. I was overwhelmed by the beauty of the different clay pots I saw all over the Tuscan countryside one spring. I wanted to find a way to bring the warm earthy beauty of these images indoors to my table. The result? This favorite table setting! I use clay pots for serving food and as containers for a wide variety of spring flowers.

You can have a field day yourself combing through the garden shop. You can even use your old clay pots—well scrubbed, of course. Just remember, the impact comes from the surprising variety of heights, shapes, and sizes of terra-cotta pots you put on the table.

The Table

Props

2 24-inch clay saucers
6-inch-wide clay pot and saucer
30 3-inch-wide clay pots and saucers
2 16-inch-wide flat glass platters
10-by-5-inch glass bowl
4 *monstera* leaves
a pastel tablecloth
watercress
alfalfa sprouts, parsley, or green leaves

This buffet meal should look like an indoor garden. Don't restrain yourself. Add one more small pot of flowers, one more unusual container to hold food. Garnish all platters with leaves or flowers. Keep dishes a simple glass or pastel so they blend well and you'll see how special this setup is.

Setup
Appetizers:
Use one 24-inch saucer to hold bread sticks, crackers, and rolls.
Use the 6-inch clay pot, lined with a plastic or glass dish to hold cheese spread. Place on saucer decorated with bed of alfalfa sprouts, parsley, or small green leaves.
Use the other 24-inch saucer for the devilled eggs. Line edges of saucer with romaine lettuce leaves. Fill in the rest of saucer with a bed of alfalfa sprouts. Place a "flower" of red-tipped lettuce in the center of the saucer and arrange the devilled eggs around it, on alfalfa bed.

Main Course:
Place potato salad in the glass bowl. If you wish, surround it with tiny clay pots of spring flowers.
Set the glass platters on the *monstera* leaves, and trim each platter with watercress.
Place the asparagus and beans on each of the glass platters. Arrange the asparagus so that the stems meet in the center of the platter. Drip the mustard sauce over the tips and garnish the stem ends with cress. Garnish the beans with julienned beets for color.

Dessert:
Use the small, 3-inch pots lined with clear plastic glasses to hold the fruit compote. Fill each pot and garnish with a sprig of fresh mint.
Place pots in saucers so guests may rest brownies and lemon bars on them.

The Centerpiece
Props
9-inch high strawberry jar
8 to 10 streamers of ivy
6 zinnias
4 dahlias
7 glass bud vials with stoppers

Never has the word centerpiece been so inappropriate! This is an all-over-piece that begins with the strawberry jar and goes wherever you want to take it. You can surround it with pots of flowers of all sizes, bunches of fresh herbs, and an assortment of terra-cotta planters—bowls, squares, rectangles.

Setup
Fill strawberry jar with soil. Plant ivy in soil in side openings.
Place 2 zinnias in each of three of the water filled vials.
Place 1 dahlia in each remaining vial.
Sink vials into openings at side of pot so that they are completely hidden in the soil and the flower does not have more than 3 inches of stem showing.
Set at center stage and arrange your other pots and food around it.

Special Touches
The children's individual Easter baskets hold their meals. Choose the standard wicker baskets with tall handles. Wrap pastel ribbons around the handles so they cover them. Tie in bow at end of handle and let ribbon trail down.

Fill the baskets with colored tissue paper and rest food wrapped in clear plastic in "nest". Add a chocolate Easter bunny and, if you want, top the basket with an Easter egg with the child's name written on it. Remember to include an oversized pastel paper napkin.

COUNTDOWN

Two Weeks Before
- ☐ Mail invitations.

Five Days Before
- ☐ Collect or buy terra-cotta serving pieces and strawberry jar.

Four Days Before
- ☐ Call guests who have not RSVP'd.
- ☐ Write out shopping list for decorations and groceries.

Three Days Before
- ☐ Buy nonperishable groceries.
- ☐ Contact florist to make sure *monstera* leaves are available. Set up strawberry jar with soil and plant ivy.

Two Days Before
- ☐ Buy fruit.
- ☐ Double check to see you have all cooking and serving pieces.

One Day Before
- ☐ Prepare potato salad. Do not add dressing. Boil eggs. Make cream cheese spread.
- ☐ Buy fresh vegetables.
- ☐ Bake lemon bars and brownies.
- ☐ Buy flowers and leaves.
- ☐ Set up basic table.

Party Day!
- ☐ Bake ham and turkey in early morning.
- ☐ Assemble deviled eggs.
- ☐ Assemble children's sandwiches.
- ☐ Add dressing to potato salad.
- ☐ Cook fresh vegetables.
- ☐ Finish table setting and arrangements.

Family Easter Dinner

Easter Sunday

Mid-afternoon

*E*aster is a quiet yet festive occasion for the family to enjoy a leisurely midday feast. But this meal does not have to be confined to Easter. You and your family deserve the chance to celebrate spring together any day of the week!

MENU

8 People

* *Ercole's Olive Appetizer*

* *Rolled Boneless Leg of Lamb with Mint Stuffing*

* *Brown Rice Exotica*

Peas with Mushrooms
Cucumber & Radish Salad

* *Bessie's Easter Pie*

SETTING THE STAGE

Easter is a time for pretty, sentimental decorations. This party appeals to the child in us all. You might like to take it one step further and spread the Easter theme throughout your house using flowers and brightly colored eggs and candies.

The Table

Props

oversized carving platter
18-inch round, white ceramic serving platter
cornflower-blue tablecloth
pale yellow cloth napkins
8 pale pastel salad plates
2 bunches fresh mint

Concentrate your efforts for this table setting on the display of the lamb and vegetables. The beautiful colors of the food are the focal point.

Setup

Place rice around outside of the serving
   platter; fill center with peas.
Arrange mint sprigs around the outside of the
   rice.
Arrange salad on plates and serve.
Set lamb on carving platter. Garnish with
   parsley.

The Centerpiece

Props

6 double handfuls of straw (available at
   nurseries, gardening shops)
8 to 10 colored Easter eggs
bag jelly beans
3 6-inch pots of daffodils (with about 5
   flowers per pot)
3 pieces of straw matting, 6 by 6 inches
5 lengths of brown twine, 12 inches long
optional:
"bird's nest," 8 inches across (available from
   florists)
4 quail eggs

Keep this arrangement "loose" and natural looking. Don't make the straw too neat or place the flowers and eggs in even rows. Think about how nature spontaneously arranges wild flowers and how the wind blows the grasses. You can't improve on that vision.

Setup

Cover table with blue cloth.

Spread straw lengthwise across table in a foot-wide swath. Let it be shaggy and textured.

Sprinkle jelly beans and colored eggs through the straw.

Cover daffodil pots with straw matting and secure it around top of pots with twine.

Place pots at irregular intervals in the straw.

Add bird's nest and quail eggs just off center in the straw.

COUNTDOWN

One Week Before
- ☐ Write out shopping list for decorations and groceries.
- ☐ Order lamb.

Four Days Before
- ☐ Buy nonperishable groceries.

Three Days Before
- ☐ Order flowers, straw.

One Day Before
- ☐ Buy fresh vegetables.
- ☐ Make olive appetizer.
- ☐ Get flowers and set-up table and centerpiece.
- ☐ Bake dessert.

Party Day!
- ☐ Prepare salad in the morning. Do not pour dressing until ready to serve.
- ☐ Time lamb so it is finished half an hour after guests arrive.
- ☐ Cook rice one hour before lamb is done. Keep warm over low flame.
- ☐ Twenty minutes before serving, cook peas.

It's Derby Day
Time For A Tailgate Picnic

at Lincoln Park
Area #47

Saturday, May 8   *1 P.M.*

RSVP

Whether you can make it to Lexington, Kentucky, or not, Derby Day is a wonderful occasion for casual celebrations. The blend of refinement and country comfort that it symbolizes lends itself to a festive gathering of friends at any park or recreation area. To organize the party, enlist the help of the other guests. You can plan the menu and choose the arrangements. You should take care of preparing the main course and appetizer but ask each guest or family to bring one of the other courses. And work with your guests on the food presentation and supplies for eating and seating.

MENU

10 People

Mint Juleps

Selection of Imported Beers

* Cheese Straws

* Honey-Batter Fried Chicken
Homemade Corned Beef

Pumpernickel & Onion Breads

Basket of Cold Mixed Vegetables
(Broccoli, Cauliflower, Zucchini Sticks,
& Cherry Tomatoes)
* Curry Dip

Macaroni Salad with Sweet Red Peppers

Emmentaler & Beaufort Cheeses

Hot Coffee with Irish Cream

Oatmeal Raisin Cookies

Invitations

Postcards of paintings of rural scenes or pictures of old cars would make funny invitations for this party. If you want to be more traditional, opt for dark green cards with matching envelopes.

SETTING THE STAGE

Blend the natural beauty of a picnic with a few glamorous touches of indoor elegance and this party becomes a special event. I love the idea of bringing silver candlesticks and serving trays, good wineglasses and utensils, and fine linen. When you set up the food on blankets on the tailgates or in the trunks of the cars, these unexpected touches make it seem like a dreamy fantasy. If you choose to be more practical—and there's no reason that has to be dull!—try to keep a cohesive color scheme and choose paper plates, serving dishes, and tablecloths that have the feel of the Kentucky bluegrass scene. I suggest hunter green plates and tartan plaid paper napkins.

The Table

Props

host supplies:
5 plaid blankets or cotton cloths in dark greens or browns to be used as tablecloths for each car's tailgate, hatchback or trunk.
dinner plates in heavy paper or china
utensils
carving knife
serving spoons and forks
brightly colored cloth napkins
silver candlesticks (if desired)

Car #1 supplies:
glasses (either crystal or clear plastic)
bottle opener
cocktail napkins

Car #2 supplies:
bread basket
platter for vegetables (silver, glass, or white china)
bowl for dip

Car #3 supplies:
plastic coffee cups
small white dessert plates (plastic, paper, or china)

Car #4 supplies:
paper napkins (as back up)
cream and sugar for coffee (in silver if
　possible)
plastic garbage bags for cleanup

Each tailgate should be set-up so that self-ser-vice is simple and mess proof. This is a lighthearted, easy-going party. You don't want to fuss. But you should use your eye to con-struct attractive presentations in any situation. Let your imagination soar. Grab some trailing vines off the trees and wind them around the serving dishes. Pick spring leaves to garnish platters. Find wild flowers or weeds to make instant bouquets. The whole world is out there waiting for you. It's the perfect opportunity to be a nature scavenger!

Setup

Park cars in a semicircle
Spread blankets over each tailgate
Have each car arrange their own food and
　dishes
As host you may make your presentation
　elaborate, using silver and china and
　decorating with vines and flowers

COUNTDOWN

Two Weeks Before
- ☐ Mail invitations.
- ☐ Confer with guests about division of responsibilities for food. Offer suggestions and finalize menu.

Five Days Before
- ☐ Assemble the supplies, blankets, serving dishes, and utensils that are host's responsibility.

Four Days Before
- ☐ Prepare cheese straws. Store in airtight container.

Two Days Before
- ☐ Call guests to see if they are having any trouble preparing their contributions or assembling their supplies.

One Day Before
- ☐ Cook chicken and corned beef.

Party Day!
- ☐ Arrive at picnic site one hour early. Clean up, arrange, and organize as much as possible before other guests arrive.
- ☐ Once all cars are there, arrange food.

FOR MOM

*for all you do
we honor you*

Happy Mother's Day
Sunday Brunch

*M*other's Day should be a day of rest, so start it off with brunch for your favorite mom. The whole family can have fun preparing it together. When my son, Brad, asked me what I'd like for Mother's Day, I replied instantly: a crowded kitchen, a festive table, and a leisurely meal.

MENU

Fresh Orange Juice

*Baked Eggs with Canadian Bacon

Hot Croissants

*Mom's Favorite Jam
(Raspberry, Apricot, or Orange
Marmalade)*

*Cinnamon Coffee

Strawberries with Sweet Heavy Cream

SETTING THE STAGE

I love the idea of having everyone in the family work together to make this brunch. When the food is prepared, put it on individual trays and carry it out to the table. But, just to surprise mom, you have arranged a centerpiece that she can take off the table and put next to her bed to remind her of your feelings all through the coming week.

The Table

Props

individual lacquer or wicker trays
pastel place mats (one for each tray)
2 yards of pastel ribbon per tray
bowl of crushed ice per juice glass
white tablecloth

The beauty of this table comes from the white cloth, the arrangement of the food on the trays, and the ribbons dancing across the tabletop.

Setup

Line each tray with a place mat.
Tie two 18-inch lengths of ribbon to each side of the tray letting it stream down from the bow or knot.
Place eggs, baked in individual ramekins, and croissants on white or pastel colored plates.
Set juice glasses in bowls filled with crushed ice. Decorate ice with flower petals, candy hearts, or slices of fresh orange if you wish.
Place individual pots of jam next to the hot croissant.

The Centerpiece

Props

Trademark flat bamboo tray
5 bud vases
5 irises or tulips
2 roses (use the petals)
10 yards of 1-inch-wide ribbon, striped, gingham, solid, polka dot, or a mixture.

The key to making this look alive is to let the natural curl of the ribbons and the random sprinkle of the rose petals create movement and texture across the tabletop. Neat and straight are dull!

Setup

Run ribbon lengthwise down table so that each piece curls at the ends.
Sprinkle rose petals over the ribbon.
Place wicker basket on ribbon at center or end of table.
Fill bud vases with irises or tulips. Place on wicker basket.

COUNTDOWN

Four Days Before
- ☐ Gather table setting supplies and centerpiece props.

Three Days Before
- ☐ Write out shopping list for decorations and groceries.
- ☐ Buy non-perishable groceries.

One Day Before
- ☐ Buy flowers.
- ☐ Buy strawberries and croissants.

Party Day!
- ☐ Set up table and trays.
- ☐ Cook and assemble meal right before serving.

A Moveable Memorial Day Cookout

Memorial Day Monday 8 P.M.

*Indoors/Outdoors
Depending on the
Weather*

RSVP

A weatherproof picnic that can go from your backyard to your porch or living room floor without any trouble at all is the perfect solution to planning a spring barbecue. You can grill the hamburgers in the garage or on the porch if it rains—or even broil them in the oven. The decorations and the planning will work wherever you set them up.

MENU

20 People

Beer on Tap

Zinfandel and Soave

Fresh Carrot & Cucumber Sticks

Fresh Herb Dip

Provolone Cheese & Genoa Salami

Grilled Hamburgers with Toppings

Grilled Bacon Bits

Shredded Cheddar Cheese

* Mary's Homemade Catsup

Sliced Beefsteak Tomatoes

Chopped Onions

Pickle Relish

German & Dijon Mustards

Pumpernickel & Sesame Buns

* Chili Beans   * Old Fashioned Coleslaw

Frozen Chocolate Bananas on Sticks

Invitations

For a really special touch, you can take plain white cards and paint them with pale water color washes that echo the same colors you are using on your stenciled tablecloth. A green felt tip pen can be used to write the information over the watercolor. And if you want to take it one step further, sprinkle a pinch of spring scented potpourri into each envelope.

SETTING THE STAGE

If you're dining outside bring all the comforts of home out to your guests. The food is simple. The graciousness comes from the special effort you make to create a pretty garden setting.

The Table

<u>Props</u>
2 picnic tables
folding table
2 pieces of canvas, 6 by 10 feet
brown cloth (for folding table)
2 Chinese bamboo steamers
large tambori table
large cast-iron pot
wooden salad bowl
acrylic paints
4 floral stencils
cushions for the picnic benches
10 votive candles

The highlight of this table is the stenciled canvas cloth. The dishes and serving pieces should coordinate with the colors on the cloth. A rustic Oriental look, not polished and lacquered but warm and woody, blends well with the cloth and the menu.

Setup

To stencil canvas:

Use acrylic paints and stencil brushes (available at any paint or decorating store) to apply floral stencils. Remember, for best results keep decorations around border and at center of the cloths.

Spread canvas on tables.

Use folding table covered with brown cloth as buffet near grills.

Set tambori table on one end. Line one bamboo steamer with glass plate. Arrange cheese and salami on plate.

Serve chili beans in cast-iron pot. Put salad in wooden bowl. Put buns in the second bamboo steamer.

The Centerpiece

Props

5 kerosene lanterns
flat of petunias
6 ivy plants

Since the impact of this table comes from the tablecloth, it is not necessary to create a complicated centerpiece. You want to bring the beauty of this spring night to the table.

Setup

Place three lanterns around on the dining tables. Turn the wicks down low so they cast a very gentle glow.

Set two lanterns on the buffet table.

Place plants next to lanterns on the buffet table.

COUNTDOWN

Two Weeks Before
- ☐ Mail invitations.
- ☐ Make catsup. Store in refrigerator.

Five Days Before
- ☐ Write out shopping list for decorations and groceries.

Four Days Before
- ☐ Stencil tablecloth
- ☐ Buy nonperishable groceries.
- ☐ Call guests who have not RSVP'd.

Three Days Before
- ☐ Buy components for table setting and centerpiece.

Two Days Before
- ☐ Prepare chili beans.

One Day Before
- ☐ Prepare coleslaw.
- ☐ Buy fresh vegetables and flowers. Buy rest of food.

Party Day!
- ☐ Set up table, buffet, and grill 2 hours before party.
- ☐ Start grill at 8 P.M. just after guests arrive.

*Too many cooks
improved this meal!*

*It's our way of saying
how we feel.*

*Love and thanks
for all you do*

Happy Father's Day

Sunday   *6:30 P.M.*

*T*his special dinner menu is designed so that the children can cook the meal. With your supervision, any child over eight should be able to be a full participant.

MENU

4 People

Dad's Favorite Beer or Wine

* *Marinated London Broil*

* *Old Fashioned Green Beans*

Baked Idaho Potato with Butter & Sour Cream

Romaine & Bibb Salad with Radishes Vinaigrette Dressing

* *Herb Buttered Italian Bread*

Coffee

* *Chocolate Chip Pecan Pie*

SETTING THE STAGE

Change the look of your dining room so it reflects the masculine flavor of a hunting lodge, den, or club. Bring in dark or deep-colored cloths, checkered place mats and napkins perhaps; use wood, brass, pewter, or ceramic dishes. This is a chance to make dad feel like the king of the roost.

The Table

Props
deep green tablecloth
cutting boards at each place for "place mats"
 (or checkered white and green place mats
 and napkins)
wooden carving board for meat

Simple, bold choices make this table look handsome. Let the kids experiment with using the housewares you have in new and different ways. Maybe they'll find a pewter creamer to use as a container for the sour cream or a gravy boat for the salad dressing!

Setup
If you use cutting boards for place mats, put
 plate on top, set silverware to side, and fold
 napkin in center of plate.
Bring London broil to table on cutting board.
 Decorate with whole mushrooms, tomato
 wedges, and parsley.

The Centerpiece

<u>Props</u>

parchment paper, 9 by 12 inches
a red silk cord, 6 inches long
photos, mementos, and newspaper clippings
   from dad's life
sheet of foam or poster board

For this occasion two homemade centerpieces
are the perfect touch.

<u>Setup</u>

Write out a menu on the parchment paper
   identifying each child's contribution to the
   meal. Roll like a scroll and tie with the
   cord. Set at Dad's place.
With the collected photos, etc., make a
   collage of the high points of his life: fishing
   trips, marriage, promotions, the birth of his
   children. Mat and frame it.

COUNTDOWN

Four Days Before
- ☐ Assemble props for table and centerpiece.
- ☐ Make centerpiece over next two days.

Three Days Before
- ☐ Write out shopping list.
- ☐ Buy nonperishable groceries.

One Day Before
- ☐ Marinate London broil.
- ☐ Make salad dressing. Store in refrigerator.
- ☐ Buy beans, vegetables, and bread.

Party Day!
- ☐ Bake pie in morning. Reheat to serve.
- ☐ Prepare salad in the morning. Pour dressing immediately before serving.
- ☐ Cook green beans *al dente* in afternoon. Reheat to serve.
- ☐ Prepare herb bread mixture in afternoon.
- ☐ One hour before serving, bake potatoes.
- ☐ Broil steak immediately before serving.
- ☐ Finish herb bread and heat immediately before serving.

Chapter Five
SUMMER DELIGHT

*S*ummer is never, never long enough! Its morning glories, afternoon pleasures, and evenings' slow descending dusks, fill us with a mixture of energy and lassitude. Life is free and breezy; the wind rustles leaves; we kick off our shoes. Small pleasures of the season are reason enough for a summer party: The first crop of vegetables, planting the first petunias, the day the pool is filled.

In the summer entertaining can be simple. Food is light and healthful, the settings echo the natural abundance that flourishes around us. The sun and moon are your romantic lighting.

You don't need to have a fixed approach to party planning. The number of guests may expand suddenly, so food and decor must be flexible, too. In the cycle of life celebrations, summer is a time for easy, effortless joys. So mix up your summer calendar with small fetes and holiday bashes.

The Plants of Summer
Summer-ize your house with natural, unfussy arrangements that grow out of the abundant excesses of Mother Nature. If you set your summer look early in the season, it can be

added to for special occasions. Don't bother with formal arrangements, they won't last in the heat, and they take too much time. Create a bounty of begonia blooms by putting pots into easily portable wooden flats Plant window boxes of geraniums for a season long splash of color. Hang baskets of moss-banked fuchsia or set boxes of fragrant herbs in your kitchen window. A single bloom of white rhododendron in a cobalt-blue vase or a bunch of daisies in a ceramic pitcher can bring the summer spirit indoors.

In the summertime, flowers and plants are in such abundance that we must make some choices or be overwhelmed! I've selected my favorite cut flowers, herbs and weeds, potted plants, and vegetables to use in arrangements and centerpieces. What are your favorites?

Tips on Arranging
Vegetables can be used in arrangements as containers for other food (a scooped-out cabbage can hold a glass bowl of cheese dip), as edible centerpieces (in an artfully arranged platter of crudités), or as a stunning still life that feeds the eyes. *Hint*: mist vegetables with water every thirty minutes to keep them

Herbs and Weeds	Cut Flowers	Potted Plants	Vegetables
Queen Anne's lace	dahlias	geraniums	cabbage
milkweed	zinnias	impatiens	brussels sprouts on stem
basil	roses	pansies	cherry tomato plants
dill	sweet peas	fuchsias	red sweet peppers
chives	marigolds	ranunculus	string beans

fresh.

Herbs and Weeds are wonderful center-pieces. An array of pots, right off the kitchen sill, set in a basket on a luncheon table is both pretty and aromatic. Roadside weeds, free for the taking, are another source of inexpensive, beautiful summer blooms. ***Hint***: when using weeds try combining them with very culti-vated flowers, such as roses, for an unusual bouquet.

Cut Flowers last in the cool of the house but can't take the summer heat if you use them at an outdoor party. The exaggerated color and shapes of summer flowers make them very effective when used singly in a bud vase or in combination with vines and branches. Try massing a large bunch of zinnias in a large pitcher. Add trailing ivy.

Potted Plants can travel from the yard to the dining table and back again. In the sum-mer I love to combine them with tomato plants, radishes, and leafy greens in a big wicker basket on my kitchen counter.

The Trademark Look

Using the trademark wicker baskets, glass bowl, and tambori tables you can create sum-mer arrangements.

Sparklers and Stripes Forever

It's Square Dancing Time

July 4th   *2 P.M.*

Come with bells on!!!
RSVP

*T*his is the most American of holidays—so go with it! Red, white, and blue are the colors of the day. A barbecue and square dancing are the perfect way to get friends and family into the spirit of '76!

MENU

40 People

Selection of American Beers

* *Barbecued Shrimp in the Shells*

French Bread

Bacon Basted Chicken   *Texas Style Ribs*

Grilled Corn in Husks   * *Creole Cabbage*

Hot Parker House Rolls

Sweet Butter   *Apple Butter*

Iced Coffee

Watermelon

* *Giant Granola Cookies*

* *Uncle Sam's Chocolate Cake*

Invitations

Send this invitation on a red card decorated with blue and silver stick-on stars. Pen the information with silver ink. Add "Come with Bells On" if you like, so all your guests will ring in the holiday while they square-dance.

SETTING THE STAGE

When you entertain outdoors, use the scenery as a backdrop. Special decorating touches and the presentation of the food unify the party setting with the natural environment. Remember: All decorating touches should be grand enough to stand out in the great out-of-doors.

The Table

Props
red oilcloth tablecloth
4 red cotton bandanas
solid white serving dishes and platters
40 deep blue oversized paper napkins
40 pieces of red ribbon or cord 6 inches long

The best way to set the food off is to keep the colors simple yet dramatic. The yellow of the corn, the pink of the shrimp, the toasty brown of the ribs and chicken will provide a lively contrast of colors and textures.

Setup
Cover buffet table with red oilcloth.
Lay the four red bandanas in a diamond
    pattern with ends overlapping slightly,
    down the length of the table.
Roll silverware in napkins. Tie each package
    together with a red ribbon or piece of cord.

The Centerpiece

Props

2 large, plain, brown paper bags
4 small brown paper sandwich bags, 10 by 5 inches
2 red geranium plants in 8-inch-wide pots; plants should be at least 12 inches high
4 red geranium plants in 4-inch-wide pots; plants should be at least 10 inches high
4 small bud vials
6 white carnations
6 bachelor's buttons
2 red ribbons, 24 inches long

Wandering through my local supermarket one day, enjoying the variety of colors and shape in the vegetable department, I noticed a shelf of geraniums. Right next to it was a huge stack of brown paper bags. Instantly I imagined the plants *inside* the bags! Why not? "Give me six plants and a stack of those bags, please," I said to the bewildered grocer. After playing around with them at home I came up with this centerpiece. It looked perfect in the backyard! This is where my ideas come from—chance events and coincidences. A roving eye is your best tool for creative entertainment ideas. So don't hesitate to try out your ideas no matter where they strike you.

Setup

Put each of the larger geraniums into a large brown bag.
Roll down the top of the bag (gently) until you have created a large cuff. You should expose the stem to within 3 inches of the soil line.
Tie one of the red ribbons around each of the bags, just below the cuff.
Put the 4 smaller geraniums into the sandwich bags.
Roll the bags down to form a cuff.
Insert three carnations or bachelor's buttons into each bud vial. Fill with water and secure stopper.
Vary the heights of the flowers from 4 to 6 to 11 inches.
Plant vials into soil (three to a pot) around the small geranium plants.
Cluster the 6 bags of flowers at one end of the table, the tall one in back.

Special Touches

If you want to go all out to make your backyard a party setting, you might want to set off the square-dancing area with banners of calico or gingham fabric (2 feet by 6 feet). Insert a dowel or thin strip of wood into a hem at top and bottom of panel. Hang panels from trees. One step further? Assemble white wicker baskets full of flowers and suspend them from tree branches, too!

COUNTDOWN

Two Weeks Before
- ☐ Mail invitations.

One Week Before
- ☐ Scout out centerpiece supplies.
- ☐ Check on cooking and serving utensils. Buy what's needed.

Five Days Before
- ☐ Write out shopping list for decorations and groceries.

Four Days Before
- ☐ Call guests who have not RSVP'd.

Three Days Before
- ☐ Buy nonperishable groceries.

Two Days Before
- ☐ Bake granola cookies. Store in airtight container.

One Day Before
- ☐ Buy flowers.
- ☐ Prepare Creole cabbage.
- ☐ Marinate shrimp.

Party Day!
- ☐ Bake cake in the morning. Keep on covered cake tray until serving time.
- ☐ Set up buffet, cooking area, and decorations in the morning.
- ☐ Time shrimp so it is ready when guests arrive.

Welcome to the Waters

at the Taylors
4–10 P.M.
July 24

Bring your suit, a towel,
& a boat to float

RSVP

Water soothes our soul and inspires our imagination. Great painters from Monet to Hockney have celebrated pools, lakes, and oceans. So this summer use the natural beauty of water to frame your festivities. You may want to have friends over to open the season at the seashore, a lakeside cottage, or your backyard pool. I've chosen a pool party to show you how simple summer entertaining can be, but you can transport this party to any locale.

The key to all these sybaritic pleasures is casual, carefree planning. Food must be easy to prepare, the decor simple and summery.

MENU

8–12 People

Chilled White Wine

Spiced Tropical Punch

Chicken Salad in Tomato Shells

Watercress & Mushroom Salad

Sourdough Bread

Gouda & White Cheddar Cheeses

Iced Tea with Fresh Mint

Watermelon

Fresh Strawberries

Pineapple

Frozen Fruit Daiquiries

Invitations

Cards with illustrations of tropical scenes, fresh fruit, or other summery images make the perfect tone setter for this party. If you are feeling particularly creative, consider sending travel brochures for tropical locales in which you have inserted a handwritten card.

SETTING THE STAGE

Light and simple decor goes with this light summer menu. You may want to set up an outdoor buffet or have guests come into the house to serve themselves. But I prefer setting up individual trays in the kitchen and bringing them out to the guests. Seconds can be passed later if needed. I think it's best to put your efforts into the presentation of the watermelon and the setup of the centerpiece.

The Table

Props
2 *monstera* leaves
deep green tablecloth
2 dozen 6-inch wooden picks

On a tea wagon or poolside table set out the watermelon so guests can help themselves. Make sure you have a good supply of napkins!

Setup
Dessert:
Place cloth on table. Top with *monstera* leaves, placed end to end.
Cut watermelon in half lengthwise. Slice individual wedges from top half. Put back on bottom half in an alternating pattern. Secure with picks.
Cut pineapple sticks. Arrange with strawberries around the edge of the watermelon (on top of the *monstera* leaves).
Garnish with sprigs of fresh mint.

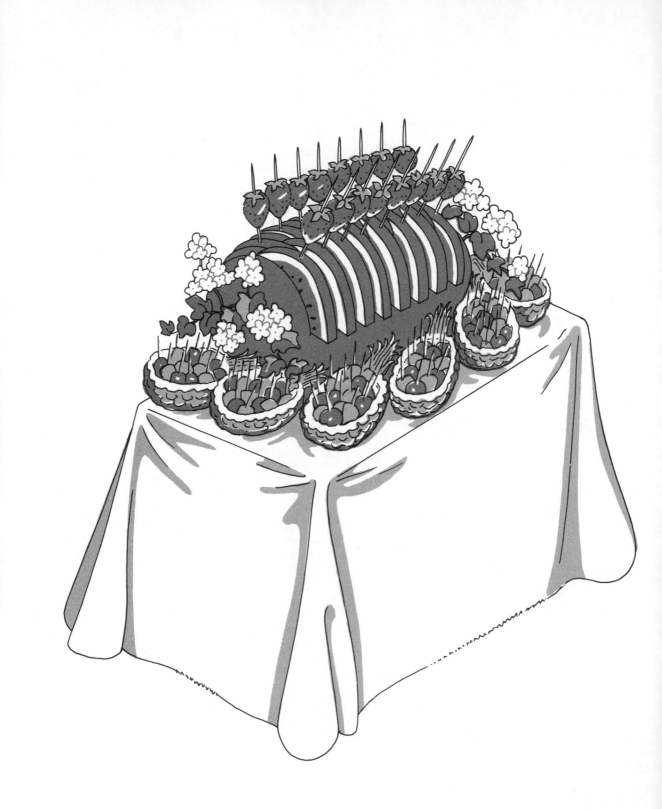

The Centerpiece

Props

Boston fern
bird's nest fern
rabbit's foot fern
3 6-inch pots of cascading geraniums
3 6-inch pots of pansies
flat of green moss, enough to cover the entire top of the basket
large wicker basket, at least 28 inches in diameter with 6-inch sides

This centerpiece is made to be placed on the ground near the edge of the pool, under a shady tree, or in the area where the deck chairs are so your guests don't have to look at the raw cement around the pool's edge!

Setup

Place wicker basket where you want it to stay.
Place ferns in basket, in a triangle.
Fill in spaces between fern pots with other flowers.
Elevate pansy pots so they are tall enough to be seen.
Fill basket with moss to cover pots to soil line.

COUNTDOWN

Two Weeks Before
- [ ] Mail invitations.

One Week Before
- [ ] Scout out basic supplies for table, centerpiece, and cooking.

Five Days Before
- [ ] Write out shopping list for decorations and groceries.

Four Days Before
- [ ] Call guests who have not RSVP'd.

Three Days Before
- [ ] Buy potted plants for centerpiece.
- [ ] Buy nonperishable groceries.

Two Days Before
- [ ] Assemble centerpiece.

One Day Before
- [ ] Buy fresh fruit and vegetables.
- [ ] Make iced tea.
- [ ] Prepare chicken salad. (Do not put in tomato shells.)

Party Day!
- [ ] Stuff tomato shells with chicken salad.
- [ ] Set up daiquiri bar.
- [ ] Cut and arrange watermelon just before serving.

Be Our Guests

Labor Day Weekend

Saturday, 11 A.M.–Sunday, 3 P.M.

RSVP

*W*eekend guests! They are a big part of the summer cycle. The Labor Day weekend is a great time to spend the last lazy days of summer with special friends. But no matter what time of year you open your home, there is a lot to pay attention to—at least two meals a day, the guests' bedroom and bath, entertainment. It can be exhausting if you don't strike a balance between organization and an easy-going spirit.

MENU

6 People

Saturday Breakfast

Fresh Orange Juice

French Roast Coffee

Blueberry Muffins & Sweet Butter

Bagels & Cream Cheese

Sweet Butter   *Cream Cheese*

Saturday Lunch

Beer

Chilled White Wine

Mixed Green Salad

* Pita Pockets stuffed with Chicken & Mozzarella

* Homemade Blueberry Tarts à la Mode

Saturday Dinner

Gewürztraminer or Chenin Blanc

Little Neck Clams on the Half Shell

* Chicken and Sausage Gumbo

Hot Fluffy Rice

Spinach & Avocado Salad

French Baguettes

Café au lait

* Génoise with Lemon Apricot Glaze

Sunday Morning Super Brunch

Aquavit Bloody Marys

* Eggs Florentine

Toasted English Muffins   *Whipped Butter*

* Autumn Apple Cake

For the Road

Miniature Monterey Jack & Bonbel Cheeses

Apples & Bananas

Sesame Breadsticks

Thermos of Hot Coffee or Cold Lemonade

Invitations

Since you will probably not be inviting more than two to four guests for the weekend, such invitations can be handled over the phone. Once plans have been set, it is a good idea to follow them up with an informal note about two weeks ahead of time confirming the plans.

SETTING THE STAGE

The weekend can be a time for you to have fun with your friends or an endless round of cooking and clean up! I don't want to be trapped in the kitchen when there's good company around, and there's no reason you should be either. Make as many of the meals self-service as possible and save yourself for a really glorious Saturday night spread.

The Table

Props

2 2-inch clam shells per person
2 large scallop shells or shell-shaped china dishes, 18 inches wide.
large white place plate per person
large scallop style *coquille* dish per person
white porcelain Chinese soup spoon per person
natural burlap tablecloth
seaweed
plastic liner to put under tablecloth
Wicker place mats or white paper fans used as place mats

The vibrantly colored bits and pieces of shells on the beach always fascinate me. The endless variety, the colors, and the texture of the sand and shells combined is what I want to bring to this table setting. If you cannot get a hold of all the shell dishes, don't despair. Use plain white or pale pink china instead and concentrate your efforts on creating the centerpiece that follows.

Setup

Spread plastic liner over dining table. Top with the natural burlap cloth.
Arrange place mats. Put two clam shells at top of each and fill with salt and pepper.
Serve clams on bed of seaweed.
Set porcelain spoon on mat. Use with the gumbo.
Fill one large scallop shell dish with gumbo.
Fill the second with rice.
Serve individual portions of gumbo in large *coquille* dishes.

The Centerpiece

Props

3 pounds of white sand
4 large scallop shells
glass hurricane cylinder, 24 inches high
1 3-inch-wide peach candle
4 to 12 flowers, cut off stems—zinnias, hibiscus, or fuchsia, for example
as many sea shells, bits of shells, coral, sea glass, or any other beachcomber's treasures as you can assemble

Bring the beach to the dining room with this seaside fantasy that will whet the appetite just like a sea breeze! The most important thing to remember is that you want a flowing, natural looking arrangement that stretches lengthwise from one end of the table to the other.

Setup

Spread sand under and around centerpiece. Place hurricane glass and candle slightly off center.

Surround base of hurricane glass with the 4 scallop shells in a cloverleaf pattern. Fill with water. Float flowers in shells.

Spread other shells down tabletop.

Don't hesitate to add flowers, votive candles, pieces of coral, even rock candy. Don't crowd the table, but give it texture and rhythm.

Special Touches

Since your guests are staying overnight it is necessary to make some gestures of welcome to make them feel at home. A special scented soap with their towels, a single rose in a bud vase by their bed, a chocolate on their pillow when they turn in for the night—any one of those touches will be warm and welcoming.

Here is a list of the kinds of little gestures you might like to extend to your guests. See what strikes you as fun to do *and* fun to receive.

Provide road maps and local tourist information for them so they can adventure on their own if they like.

Set out a bucket of ice and a pitcher of water (or other drinks) by their bed.

Give them their own house keys.

Put a supply of current magazines for their nighttime reading in their rooms.

Give them a written schedule of the weekend's events if you are planning on doing a lot of socializing.

If you do not have a second bathroom, label the guest towels so they know which to use.

Set out a little kit of toiletry supplies in case they have forgotten anything.

COUNTDOWN

Two Weeks Before
- ☐ Mail invitations.

One Week Before
- ☐ Write out shopping list for all groceries for weekend.
- ☐ Write out complete decorations and tablesetting list.

Five Days Before
- ☐ Begin assembling centerpiece and table-setting supplies.
- ☐ Buy non-perishable groceries.

Four Days Before
- ☐ Finish shopping and assembling supplies.

Two Days Before
- ☐ Bake chicken breasts. Refrigerate until ready to slice for Saturday lunch.

One Day Before
- ☐ Prepare autumn apple cake for Sunday brunch. Store in airtight container.
- ☐ Prepare gumbo. Store in refrigerator.
- ☐ Bake *génoise* cake. Do not glaze. Store in airtight container.

Party Days!

Saturday Lunch

- ☐ Prepare blueberry tarts in the morning. Reserve ice cream until served.
- ☐ Buy or cut flowers for arrangements.

Saturday Dinner

- ☐ Set up dinner table and centerpiece in afternoon. Glaze cake in afternoon.

Sunday Brunch

- ☐ Prepare eggs immediately before serving.

Chapter Six

AUTUMN ACTIVITIES

*T*he cool nights of autumn are a welcome change from the sweltering days of summer. The air is clear and the colors bright. It is almost beautiful enough to make us forget the approaching chill of winter. These sparkling months usher in the big entertaining season. Friends are back in town from their vacations, the kids are in school, and we busy ourselves with thoughts about the upcoming holidays.

September, October, and the beginning of November are splendid times to entertain. As the temperature falls we can return to cooking heartier food. Apple pies sweeten the air, crisp duck delights the eye, hot cider and cocoa warm the body and soul. When the world puts on a show of vibrant colors, it's time to let your cycle of celebrations be vibrant, too.

The Plants of Autumn

Late blooming flowers, vivid tree branches, the roadside wonders of dried cattails and tall pampas grass, and the colorful varieties of gourds, squashes, pumpkins, and other vegetables can be displayed to create a seasonal feeling throughout your house.

The kinds and textures of autumn's plants are more varied and richly colored than any other time of the year. I use branches, weeds, vegetables, and cut flowers to create my fall arrangements.

Tips on Arranging

Branches in early autumn bring vivid green indoors. I like to combine rhododendron, mountain laurel, eucalyptus , and *podocarpus* in a tall vase or wicker basket lined with a glass vase. As the colors change outside, replace your green branches with the red and orange branches of oak and maple. *Hint*: fall leaves stay fresh and bright for only two to three days.

Vegetables from the fall harvest can be used as containers for food. Hollow out a pumpkin and use it as a tureen for pumpkin soup or as a "vase" for an arrangement of dried pods, mums, and colored leaves. Carve out the top of an eggplant, artichoke, or red bell pepper and sink a votive candle and holder in it, or use the holders as nut cups. Combine apples studded with cloves, nuts, cinnamon sticks, and whole nutmegs with rover mums and bit-

Branches	Weeds	Vegetables	Flowers
mountain laurel	cattails	pumpkins	hydrangeas
rhododendron	milkweed	gourds	heather
fall tree branches	bittersweet	eggplant	Peruvian lillies
(maple, oak,	pokeweed	apples	chrysanthemums
etc.)	dried pods	persimmons	(spider, rover,
eucalyptus		artichokes	daisy)
podocarpus			cockscomb
			asters

tersweet berries in a large wooden bowl to form still life displays. Colorful gourds can decorate the base of any potted plant. **Hint**: to keep vegetables shiny and fresh, spray lightly with cooking oil.

Flowers are precious in the fall for they are soon to disappear with winter's approach. Masses of dried hydrangeas in a mauve basket, a single lily placed in a bud vial inserted into a carved out pear, or an eggplant filled with pink carnations create a fall look.

Weeds are yours for the picking along any roadside in America. They can be used in combination with cut flowers, by themselves, or with colorful gourds and autumn vegetables. They dry well and can last for weeks. To keep even longer, spray them with clear charcoal fixer or clear polymer.

The Trademark Look

Using the trademark wicker basket, four glass liners from the small wicker baskets, and the tallest bud vase, you can create autumn arrangements easily.

Autumn Wine Tasting

at
Ava and Paul's

7 P.M. October 3rd

Please bring a bottle of
your favorite wine

(Not necessarily the
most expensive!)

RSVP

*T*o launch the fall entertaining season, bring your friends together for an informal, fun wine tasting. Get everyone into the act! Ask each guest or couple to bring a favorite wine. This is an ideal celebration for a weekend afternoon or an early evening cocktail party.

MENU

12 People

Assorted Cheeses
(Vermont Cheddar, Brie, Havarti with
Dill, Jarlsberg, Montrachet)

A Variety of Breads
(Rye, Pumpernickel, Sour Dough, French
Baguettes)

Green & Red Grapes

Invitations

Wine labels make the perfect invitation for this party. You can assemble your own collection from bottles and mount them on card stock. Pen the invitation information on the back. If labels are hard to find, I suggest a deep burgundy colored card or a reproduction of a Greek or Roman banquet scene.

SETTING THE STAGE

A simple, edible centerpiece is the perfect backdrop for the display of wine bottles that are the focus of this setting. The rich reds and warm golden hues of the wine, combined with a bounty of breads and cheeses create a foolproof setting for a relaxed, enjoyable party.

The Table

Props

3 wine glasses per guest
36 plastic wine glasses to have on hand for backup
snack table
white linen tablecloth
large tambori table
1 small tambori table
4 burgundy, 18-inch oversized napkins for use as tambori tablecloths and to cover snack table
12 glass salad plates
12 white cloth napkins

The look here is very simple. Its beauty comes from the artful arrangement of the basic elements of the wine tasting.

Setup

Cover snack table with cloth.
Place the wine glasses on a diagonal on the snack table. Place the table at the side of the buffet.
Cover buffet with tablecloth.
Place the tambori tables on right side of buffet. Cover with the burgundy napkins.
Set out opened wine bottles on tambori tables and to the side of them.
Put serving plates and napkins at opposite end of table.

The Centerpiece

Props

2 wreath-shaped loaves of bread (any color)
2 large loaves of sourdough bread
4 baguettes
round loaf of pumpernickel
2 pounds each white and red grapes
   (minimum)
4 wooden cutting boards for bread
3 glass bowls, 8 inches in diameter
12 white votive candles
pair grape scissors
3 small wooden cheese boards
square wicker tray
wicker basket
tambori table
6 feet of grape vine
bunch bittersweet berries
6 pears
6 apples

The centerpiece is constructed of the bread *and* the food that you are serving. If your buffet is not at least five feet long, place the wine service on a separate table and make the main table for food only.

Setup

Cut the wreath-shaped loaves to form a chain. Place them at the center of the table.
Hollow out centers of sourdough loaves.
Cut Cheddar and Jarlsberg cheese into cubes. Fill hollows of bread with cheese.
Put sourdough loaves on either side of the chain.
Set one large tambori table behind the cloverleaf. Cover with square wicker tray.
Set wicker basket in back left-hand corner of tray. Fill with baguettes. Garnish with berries.
Pile grapes around basket and covering tray. Let some hang down over the edge of the tray and fall to the table below. Set fruit in the middle of the grapes.
Weave 1 and 2 foot length of vine around grapes, tray, and tambori table. Tie grapes to vine with floral wire.
Arrange remaining cheese and bread on wooden boards around bread chain.
Surround finished display with votive candles that follow the curve of the breads.
Remember to have bread and cheese knives and scissors for the grapes.

COUNTDOWN

Two Weeks Before
- ☐ Mail invitations.

One Week Before
- ☐ Scout out basic serving and table setting supplies.

Five Days Before
- ☐ Write out shopping list for decorations and groceries.
- ☐ Buy supplies.

Four Days Before
- ☐ Call guests who have not RSVP'd.

One Day Before
- ☐ Buy cheese and fruit.
- ☐ Buy bittersweet berries.

Party Day!
- ☐ Buy bread.
- ☐ Leave out cheese to soften in the morning.
- ☐ Set up centerpiece in late afternoon.

Shine On Harvest Moon!

A Dinner Party

October 21   *8 P.M.*

RSVP

A splendid autumnal dinner party with a touch of elegance gives you and your guests a chance to dress up for a special evening designed to bring out the best of this time of year.

MENU

6 People

Johannisberg Riesling or Zinfandel (a White or Red Wine)

* *Artichoke Bisque*

* *Crown Roast of Pork*

Parsleyed New Potatoes

Glazed Carrots   * *Baked Onions*

Fresh Spinach & Boston Lettuce with Mustard Vinaigrette

* *Crème de Cassis Parfaits*   *Champagne*
Cookies

Coffee

Cognac

Invitations

Send a beautiful parchment invitation. You can buy parchment at any art supply store. For the best look, have a calligrapher write out all the information. If you can't locate one, use your best script and a fine-tipped pen with brown ink.

SETTING THE STAGE

Hearty greens, deep oranges, cinnabars, and browns radiate in the candlelit glow that surrounds this handsome feast. I like to have dinners like this with my best friends because when guests know each other well, there is a warmth that takes the chill out of the air and makes the rich decor glow like real gold.

The Table

Props

2 copper bowls
deep red tablecloth
large ironstone or ceramic patterned platter
6 brass candlesticks, various heights
6 white tapers
6 wooden salad bowls
6 daisy mums
2 clementine oranges

Keep the table simple. Let the colors of the tablecloth, the food, and dishes set the tone. If you don't have brass and copper, you can use silver and white ceramic serving dishes and glass plates.

Setup

Cover table with cloth.
Serve new potatoes and salad in copper bowls. Garnish rims with red tipped lettuce leaves.
Place candlesticks with white tapers in a group just off center of the table.
Set crown roast on platter. Garnish edges of platter with glazed carrots and onions.
Garnish each "leg" of roast with a kumquat.
Scoop out two clementines leaving opening of 1½ inches at top. Fill with daisy mums. Set on side of platter.

The Centerpiece

Props

3 small ramekins, 3 inches in diameter
soufflé dish with fluted sides
styrofoam ball, 6 inches in diameter (flower
    arranger)
3 styrofoam balls, 3 inches in diameter
4 manzanita branches, three 6 inches long,
    one 1 foot long
boxwood leaves
2 pounds very small new potatoes
2 heads of red tipped lettuce
½ pound fresh red chile peppers
½ pound snow pea pods
 styrofoam sufficient to fill each ramekin and
    the soufflé dish

These autumn "trees" take time to make but
the look is truly worth the effort. The twisted
stalks of the manzanita give rhythm to the arrangement; the vegetables echo fall's colors.

Setup

Fill ramekins and soufflé dish with a cube of
    styrofoam each.
Insert the 6-inch-long branches in the small
    ramekins. Put the long branch in the
    soufflé dish.
Cover each styrofoam ball with boxwood
    leaves. Secure with toothpicks.
Set boxwood-covered balls on branches to
    form treetops. The large ball goes on the
    longest branch that is in the soufflé dish.
Toothpick chili peppers and snow pea pods
    on to styrofoam ball treetops. (Use one
    type of vegetable per tree.)
Fill the base of each ramekin with a layer of
    new potatoes. If you can't find new
    potatoes use brown or white gravel.
Fill in the base of the soufflé dish with red
    tipped lettuce.
Set trees on table in an asymmetrical pattern
    around candles and food.

COUNTDOWN

Two Weeks Before
- [ ] Mail invitations.

One Week Before
- [ ] Write out shopping list for centerpiece. Assemble supplies, except for fresh vegetables.

Five Days Before
- [ ] Write out shopping list for groceries.

Four Days Before
- [ ] Call guests who have not RSVP'd.

Three Days Before
- [ ] Buy all nonperishable groceries.

Two Days Before
- [ ] Make parfaits. Store covered in freezer.
- [ ] Start centerpieces.

One Day Before
- [ ] Buy fresh vegetables for menu and centerpiece.
- [ ] Prepare artichoke bisque. Store covered. Serve chilled or reheat.

Party Day!
- [ ] Set up table in morning.
- [ ] Prepare salad in morning.
- [ ] Buy flowers for garnishes.
- [ ] Begin roast about 4 P.M.
- [ ] An hour before dinner, cook vegetables.

*H*alloween can be fun even for grown-ups! This evening you can transform your house into a mini-disco. Let your party be loose but surprising, touched with humor and a bit of the macabre. And remember, these tips for setting up a dancing party can be used all year round.

MENU

30 People

Beer

* Fish House Punch

*Deli Salad Tray (Potato Salad,
Coleslaw, Relishes, etc.)*

*Deli Meat Platter (Beef, Pastrami,
Turkey, Salami)*

*Deli Cheese Platter (Muenster, Swiss,
Provolone, Cheddar)*

*Basket of Pumpernickel, Peasant, &
Sourdough Breads*

Horseradish, Mustards, Mayonnaise

Coffee

Basket of Apples

Spice Cupcakes

Invitations

Send out invitations written on an orange card attached with a black cord to a simple Lone Ranger mask.

Lots of people dislike costume parties. But at Halloween we're tempted to give it a try. My suggestion is to go for the middle ground. Tell the guests to come wearing the mask you've sent. You can also suggest on the invitation that they come with some prop—shawl, sari, hat, or funny shoes. That way a full costume isn't required, and those who opt out won't feel conspicuous.

SETTING THE STAGE

From the front door to the buffet, the dance floor to the bathroom, this is a night to spread the decorations and spirit throughout the house. Halloween decorations are plentiful and not too expensive. Paper bats, crepe paper streamers, bowls of candy corn, and flickering black candles can be used in abundance.

The Table

Props

6-foot-long paper skeleton (black and white)
large head of leafy green cabbage
Mylar "curtain"
4 small glass bowls, 3 inches in diameter
2 large glass fruit bowls

This buffet meal is really fun to assemble. Let your most inventive and creative impulses find expression in this one! I got this idea when I visited my son's school room at Halloween. When I saw the paper skeleton hanging on the wall I thought it would be great to use it on a Halloween dinner buffet.

Setup

Cover table or buffet with silver Mylar curtain. They come in 4 by 6 foot lengths at most party supply stores. Sometimes they are cut into wide strips. That works well, but you have to tape the strips down to the tabletop.

Place paper skeleton on Mylar.

Carve out cabbage head so a glass bowl containing potato salad can be set into it.

Put cabbage on head of skeleton. Decorate potato salad with olives, strips of pimentos, and other vegetables to create a face.

Roll up deli meats and secure with toothpicks.

Arrange deli meats on torso of skeleton. Follow shape of ribs.

Fill glass bowl with coleslaw, place on stomach.

Put bread slices down both arms.

Set a small glass bowl filled with mayonnaise and mustard at each elbow.

Leave paper hands uncovered.

Put cheese slices down both legs.

Set a small bowl of mustard and mayonnaise at each knee.

Add any details or decorations using food that you wish.

As evening goes on, fill skeleton in with fresh food.

The Centerpiece

Props

5 long black tapers

5 to 7 gourds and squashes of various shapes and sizes; for example, winter squash, turban squash, crookneck squash, Hubbard, spaghetti, acorn

2 bags of candy corn

4 small black trick-or-treat bags

2 scary rubber masks

Since the food is so integral to the look of the party, this centerpiece is simply a backdrop for the skeleton. Using the autumn vegetables brings color and texture to the table.

Setup

Arrange the gourds on the back of the buffet to one side.

Place larger gourds in center and cluster smaller ones around.

Put black candles around the vegetables.

Fill trick-or-treat bags with candy corn.

Put in the front of the vegetables.

Extra oomph? Take two large rubber masks. Stuff them with tissue paper so they stand up. Set on table near the head of the skeleton.

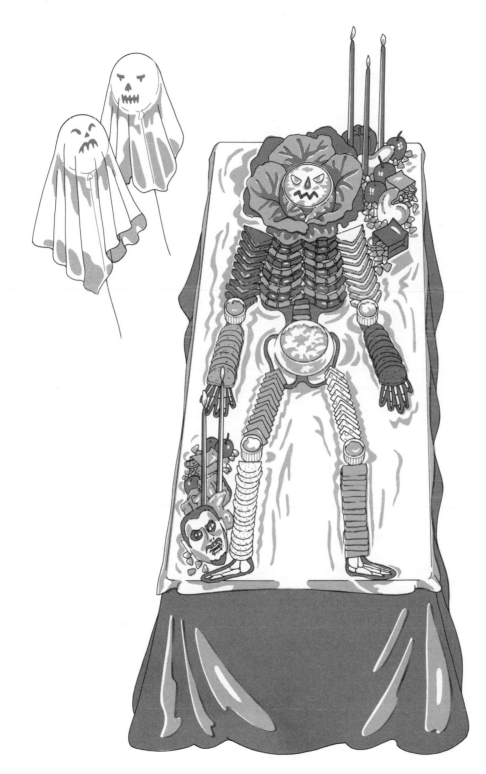

Special Touches

Dancing is great fun, but not everyone enjoys it, so you want to create a disco environment that is casual enough to let nondancers have a good time yet glitzy enough to really set the stage. The living room is the natural place for the dance floor, since in most homes it is the largest room. You'll have to remove most of the furniture. I always set aside one room for conversation—a bedroom or den with chairs and tables. Decorate the tables with black cloths, candles, and small trick-or-treat bags filled with candy. Put the living room furniture into your "quiet room" and drape it with white or black sheets or cover with black plastic trash bags.

Props for Dance Area

Decorations:
20 paper bats
clear nylon cord
6 rolls each black and orange crêpe paper
5 large pumpkins
6 stalks of corn

Lighting: special effects:
black lights, gel covered spots, mirrored balls
pink bulbs to use in your lamps
black votive candles (as many as you want)

Setup

Hang a piece of nylon cord at ceiling height the length of each wall.
Attach strips of crepe paper (alternating orange and black) from the cord to form a solid curtain.

Hang paper bats from ceiling using the same cord. Keep them above head level.
Set up the pumpkins and corn in a corner. Use pumpkins to support corn.
Add any extra Halloween decorations you like, perhaps another skeleton, paper witches, whatever strikes your fancy.

Once you have the basic dance area set up, you can bring in the lighting effects. If you wish, rent spots, gels, strobes, and mirrored balls from a theatrical lighting company. If you don't want to go to that trouble, simply put pink lightbulbs into your own lamps and drape the shades with black cloth to dim the glow.

Additional Props

5 squares white sheer synthetic fabric, 50 by 50 inches
5 helium balloons
assortment of colored Magic Markers

Setup

Draw two faces on each fabric panel—witchy or devilish.
Drape fabric over balloon. Attach 3-foot-long black string to balloon.
Let it float to the ceiling.

One more special touch you might all have fun with is to set up a face painting table where guests can decorate themselves with colors, sequins, decals, and feathers if they find they've really caught the Halloween spirit and wish they had a costume after all.

COUNTDOWN

Two Weeks Before
- [ ] Mail invitations.

One Week Before
- [ ] Write out shopping list of supplies for dance floor, centerpiece, and serving pieces.

Five Days Before
- [ ] Continue assembling props.

Four Days Before
- [ ] Call guests who have not RSVP'd.

Three Days Before
- [ ] Arrange with deli for delivery of meats, cheeses, and condiments on party day.
- [ ] Prepare music tapes or records for dancing.

Two Days Before
- [ ] Set up basic buffet and dance area.

One Day Before
- [ ] Assemble centerpiece.

Party Day!
- [ ] Make punch.
- [ ] Put together skeleton about four hours before party. Cover with plastic wrap.

Join With Us to
Give Thanks for All Our
Wonderful Friends

Thanksgiving Day

4 P.M.

*T*his favorite of all calendar holidays has a special feeling of warmth and tradition. The menu is repeated year after year, yet we never tire of the turkey or the pumpkin pie. This year, keep those old standbys alive by introducing a few new flavor surprises and making the presentation and table setting really special.

MENU

16 People

California Cabernet or French Alsatian Red or White

* Vegetable Pâté   Pumpernickel Rounds

* Turkey with
* Cornbread-Sausage Stuffing

Cauliflower au Gratin   Tiny New Peas

* Sweet Potato Soufflé

* Molded Cranberry Apple Salad

Cloverleaf Rolls   Sweet Butter

Vienna Roast Coffee

Walnut Pecan Pie

Amaretto Cookies

Invitations

Invitations to such special holidays are not usually sent out without having first talked over the arrangements with the guests. Since there is usually some discussion of whose house dinner will be held at and how the menu will be prepared, speak to your friends a few weeks ahead of time; see what their plans are. Once you've made the phone calls and set the plan, it is nice to follow up with confirming invitations, however. I like simple cards trimmed in bright Autumn colors.

SETTING THE STAGE

Thanksgiving is my favorite holiday. The food, the decor, the family spirit are all so wonderful. I can never resist going all out and making the whole house part of the celebration.

The Table

Props
3 feet of cranberry garland
16 salad plates
16 lemon leaves
2 wreaths of grapevine, 3 inches high, 14 inches in diameter
16 lady apples
16 white name cards
16 radish flowers or fluted mushrooms
16 dessert plates
16 liquor glasses
maple sugar flowers
Amaretto cookies

Garnish all your dishes with fall leaves, deep green parsley, and vivid red berries, and the table will look as good as it smells! Use your best old linen and lace on the table.

Setup

Appetizer:

Set individual sliced portions of pâté on salad
plate. Garnish with lemon leaf topped with
a small flower bud, radish flower, or carved
mushroom.

Set this plate on place plate at each setting.
Have it on the table before guests are
seated.

Main Course:

String cranberries on a thread three and one
half feet long. Tie ends together to make a
circle.

Before you bring the turkey to the table, loop
garland of cranberries around it.

Place grapevine wreaths around sweet potato
soufflé and cauliflower au gratin casseroles.

Insert a name card in slit in each lady apple.
Set one apple at each place setting.

Dessert:

Serve pie on individual dessert plates.
Garnish with maple sugar flower and two
amaretto cookies. Offer coffee with dessert.

The Centerpiece

Props

pumpkin, 16 inches high
stalk of brussels sprouts on the stem
4 ears of Indian corn
6 small gourds
5 chrysanthemums
2 orange tiger lilies
5 to 7 stalks of dried milkweed pods or other
weeds
large eggplant
4 pheasant feathers
package of cranberries
green bell pepper
bag mixed nuts
head of purple cabbage with leaves or a
purple or white cauliflower with outer
leaves
medium size tambori table
large flat wicker tray

This arrangement can go from the table to the
front hall or mantel after dinner is over. It will
last several days, and when the fresh vegetables begin to wilt, simply remove them and
keep the dried plants and gourds till the season's end.

Setup

Place pumpkin on tambori table.

Rest brussels sprout stalk on one side. Place
two ears of Indian corn alongside the
sprouts.

Put leafy cabbage or cauliflower against base
of tambori table.

Using an ice pick, jab eight holes at uneven
intervals into the top and front sides of the
pumpkin.

Insert flowers, dried weeds, and feathers into
holes.

Put two ears of Indian corn, the eggplant, and
bell pepper to the left of the cabbage.
Place gourds around corn, eggplant, and
pepper.

Sprinkle nuts and cranberries all around.

Special Touches

There are so many decorating touches you can put around the house to make it look special during this holiday time. I have two favorites: a wreath made of bittersweet and wisteria vine for the front door, and piles of colorful gourds and pumpkins placed around all my potted plants and trees.

To make the wreath, start with four 6-foot-long wisteria vines. Twist them together and form a circle. Secure with very thin wire or clear plastic thread. Wire on berries. And remember you can take this from the front door to the table if you need an instant centerpiece. Just fill the center with fall fruit, candles, or flowers.

COUNTDOWN

Two Weeks Before
- ☐ If serving fresh turkey, order now.
- ☐ Send out invitations.

One Week Before
- ☐ Make shopping list for decorations and groceries.

Five Days Before
- ☐ Check all serving pieces; buy what's needed.

Four Days Before
- ☐ Buy nonperishable groceries.

Three Days Before
- ☐ Buy nonperishable centerpiece supplies.

Two Days Before
- ☐ Buy vegetables.

One Day Before
- ☐ Bake walnut pie. Loosely cover with wax paper and store at room temperature.
- ☐ Prepare vegetable pâté. Refrigerate.
- ☐ Prepare cranberry salad.
- ☐ Buy flowers for centerpiece. Assemble centerpiece.
- ☐ If using frozen turkey allow to thaw overnight.

Party Day!
- ☐ Make radish flowers, string cranberry garland in morning.
- ☐ In early morning, prepare stuffing and stuff bird. Roast turkey.
- ☐ Set table and put on decorations.
- ☐ Make sweet potato soufflé.
- ☐ Add sour cream garnish to cranberry salad.
- ☐ An hour before serving, cook vegetables.

Chapter Seven
CELEBRATIONS OF WINTER

Winter is a time of contrasts—of bone-chilling winds and the glowing hearth; of barren trees and the vibrant beauty of a snow-covered hill. We fill our lives with tokens of comfort and joy to compensate for the seasonal deprivation of the earth. No wonder November to February marks the height of the entertainment season. What better time to bring friends together! Enjoy the best of the season—the smell of cloves, the inviting texture of quilts, and the vibrant colors of red and green and deep country tones of blue and maroon and forest green. When the senses are filled with tantalizing aromas, sights, and sounds, we feel less confined.

In this chapter we explore different Christmas celebrations from a gala feast to a cozy dinner for two, including a Christmas picnic and, of course, the traditional family dinner. Additionally, there is a dessert-laden holiday open house, an intimate New Year's dinner, a Super Bowl party, and a romantic Valentine's Day get-together.

The Plants of Winter
In winter we get the double benefit of the dramatic beauty of holly, pine branches and cones, myrtle, and early blooming bulbs such as the amaryllis, hyacinth, and narcissus. Primroses, orchids, cyclamen, azaleas, *kalanchoe,* and Christmas cactus all are available.

My favorites include seasonal branches and garlands, forced bulbs and potted plants, and special scents and accents.

Tips on Arranging
Branches of pine and holly can be used in tall vases or draped across a mantel or coffee table in a horizontal arrangement. The white birch branches can stand alone when "planted" into a clay pot painted red or gold, and filled with oasis. Cover the oasis with short sprigs of pine, moss, or pine cones. Garlands can accent your mantel, door frames, banisters, or party tables.

Bulbs and flowers in winter are such a treasure that one single bloom or pot can seem like a garden full of summer flowers. A stalk of

Branches/Garlands	Forced Bulbs/Potted Plants	Scents and Accents
pine boughs	amaryllis	cinnamon sticks
holly	azaleas	cloves
birch	cymbidium orchid	pine incense
ponderosa pine	narcissus	scented candles
laurel	hyacinths	dried flower potpourri

amaryllis in a clay pot needs no other decoration. Narcissus grouped in a flat or a pot is my favorite bedside winter flower. *Hint*: the dry air in winter is hard on plants. Mist them frequently and make sure they are watered every three days.

Scents and accents are the perfect compliment to any winter decoration. Stud apples or persimmons with cloves and set in a wooden bowl lined with spruce needles. Set on the coffee table. The aroma will fill the room. Or use pine incense placed in the base of your houseplants or trees. Cinnamon sticks or apples boiling in a pot on the stove scent the whole house.

The Trademark Look

Using the trademark moss, glass bowl, and laquered stand, you can create unexpected holiday arrangements. These two are my very favorite Christmas looks. The wisteria vine basket is filled with Spanish moss. One pot of flowers—I love orchids but azaleas or narcissus are also beautiful—is all that's needed. The glass bowl, filled with cranberries and placed upon the lacquered stand, holds hyacinth, amaryllis, and narcissus.

Alternative Christmas Trees

The Christmas tree is one tradition that can endure change. I love to create unusual decorations for my trees. It adds an element of surprise to the look of the living room and gives my family a chance to experiment with new trimming ideas. It's a tradition in my house not to have a traditional tree! This all started when we moved just before Christmas one year and didn't have our boxes of ornaments yet. What did we do? We created an edible tree.

Little straw baskets are filled with Christmas candies—chocolate kisses, peppermints, gum drops, and sugarplums. They're tied to the branches with gingham ribbons. Gingerbread men and sugar cookies in various Christmas shapes are tied with clear cord. Popcorn garlands festoon the tree, and candy canes give it added color. You can even add candied fruits. Just thread a needle and sew a loop onto each piece. Since that first year, I have used this idea again. For a holiday party I decorated a small three-foot tabletop tree with edible goodies and had guests help themselves!

Other splendid alternatives include a shell tree, an Oriental fan tree, non-tree trees, and small forests!

The Shell Tree
Tie pink cord to sand dollars, starfish, and bits of coral, and hang them on the tree. Use strings of fake pearls and garlands of pink and white beads. Glue tiny shells onto inch-wide lengths of pink ribbons, and swag the tree with them. Add tiny white lights, and you've got it!

The Oriental Fan Tree
Buy fifty 3-inch-tall red paper fans. Hang them, unfurled, all over the tree. Add strings of tiny white or red lights.

Non-Tree Trees
Non-tree trees are made from pine boughs, white birch branches, or boughs of holly. Place them in large vases or fill red-paper-covered clay pots with oasis and "plant" stems in pot. Decorate with lights and ornaments and set on coffee table, mantel, or by the front door.

The Small Forest
It is very beautiful to get three or four live pine trees ranging from 2 to 5 feet tall and cluster them together in a small forest in the corner of a room. Wrap their pots in natural burlap and secure with brown twine. Add strands of small white lights if you wish.

> *You are cordially invited*
> *to*
>
> ## A Greek Holiday Buffet
>
> *Saturday, December 19*
>
> *8 P.M.*
>
> *RSVP*

*T*his feast is perfect for the week before Christmas when you want to gather all your friends and family around you. Since some people cannot be with you on Christmas eve or day, this is a wonderful chance to share your affection with those near and dear.

Remember, the holiday season fills up social calendars, so plan this one early . . . and get invitations out at least three weeks in advance.

MENU

30 People

Demestica, Napa, Gamay Wines

* *Taramásalata*

* *Leg of Lamb Mediterranean*

* *Zucchini with Kasséri Cheese*

Hot Rice with Toasted Pine Nuts

Greek Salad with * *Garlic Dressing*

Warm Pita Bread

* *Baklava*

Coffee

Ouzo

Invitations

Blue cards with gold or silver ink or any card of a Byzantine painting make the perfect invitation for this evening.

SETTING THE STAGE

The whole house should be filled with the sumptuous glamour of this Greek buffet. And all it takes is a few well-planned decorating touches. To set the tone, we forgo the traditional red and green Christmas colors in favor of the rich and subdued Byzantine colors: dark blue, deep claret, and sparkling white and gold.

The Table

Props

deep blue tablecloth (satin if possible)
white cloth napkins rolled around silverware and tied with gold cord
100 silver paper leaves (available at party goods stores)
4 large eggplants
large carving tray (silver if possible)
3 tambori tables
3 large deep blue squares of fabric—large enough to cover tambori tables completely

This is a buffet that requires you rent dishes, silverware, and wine glasses. Select plain glass service, white napkins, and slightly ornate flatware. You can't really do the food justice with paper, plastic, or a mixture of china. If you have the space and inclination you can set up dining tables. Rent 60-inch rounds and cover them with cloths made from 120-inch pieces of gold lamé fabric. If you are having a stand-up or sit-where-you-can buffet, use some snack trays draped in gold or blue cloth to provide more places for guests to perch.

Setup

Cover buffet table with blue cloth.
Cut the top third off each eggplant. Cut bottom so it is flat and they can stand upright.
Scoop out inside of eggplant. Fill with *taramásalata*
Place eggplants on glass platter lined with silver paper leaves.

Surround with triangles of pita rounds
   arranged in a geometric pattern.
Decorate rice and zucchini dishes with silver
   leaves.
Place glass plate covered with gold doily on
   each tambori table.
Set tables to right of center. Top with rice
   and zucchini casseroles.
Set Greek salad and individual salad bowls
   (all glass) next to rice.
Set lamb on cutting board, and set board on a
   bed of silver leaves.
Place dinner plates and utensils on far end of
   buffet.

The Centerpiece

Props

8 stems of white-painted branches, 5 feet tall
4 large clay pots filled with oasis or cubes of
   Styrofoam
tambori table
gold lamé cloth to cover tambori table
5 votive candles in glass holders
artichoke
pomegranate
pineapple
eggplant
magnolia branch
a dozen walnuts
4 pots of white azaleas
2 pots of narcissus
can gold spray paint
can silver spray paint

This centerpiece is a fantasy of gold and silver
framed by a stand of white branches that runs
along the back of the buffet. The whole look
should be as lavish and rich as possible.

Setup

Pull buffet table out 6 inches from the wall.
Plant branches in Styrofoam in clay pots.
Set on floor behind buffet in a row.
Make sure tablecloth is long enough so that
   you can't see the pots from any angle.
Spray artichoke, pomegranate, magnolia
   branch, walnuts, and eggplant gold and
   silver.
Place tambori table draped with cloth to the
   right of center toward the back of the table.
Set pineapple on tambori table. Surround
   with half the walnuts.
Place magnolia branch on tambori table at
   angle so it trails down to buffet.
Set artichoke next to branch on the tambori
   table.
Add other sprayed vegetables and walnuts on
   buffet around tambori table.
Fill in spaces with silver paper leaves.
Place votive candles on tambori and buffet.
Spray azaleas and narcissus pots gold. Set on
   end of table away from the tambori table
   holding the gold and silver vegetables.

The Trademark Collection

Sparklers and Stripes Forever
Fourth of July Barbeque

Greek Holiday Buffet

The First and Finest Anniversary

**Have a Heart
Valentine's Day Dessert Party**

Mother's Day Brunch

Thanksgiving Feast

Moving In Party

Superbowl Sunday Fiesta

Spring/Summer Wedding Tea

COUNTDOWN

Three Weeks Before
- [ ] Mail invitations.

One Week Before
- [ ] Make baklava. Store in cool place in airtight container.

Five Days Before
- [ ] Write out shopping list for rest of groceries.
- [ ] Write list for decorations, serving pieces, and table setting supplies.

Four Days Before
- [ ] Call guests who have not RSVP'd.

Three Days Before
- [ ] Buy nonperishable groceries and decorations.
- [ ] Buy and spray centerpiece decorations.

Two Days Before
- [ ] Set up basic decor—arrange branches, sprayed fruit, etc.

One Day Before
- [ ] Make *taramásalata*
- [ ] Make garlic dressing.
- [ ] Buy all fresh food and flowers.

Party Day!
- [ ] Finish decorations and buffet setup.
- [ ] Cook lamb so it is ready to serve about 45 minutes after guests arrive.

Christmas Feast

*a traditional meal
for the
whole family*

Christmas Day

2 P.M.   *RSVP*

*T*he nostalgic warmth of a full-scale family Christmas is one of life's great pleasures. No need to hold back here. The blend of elegance with the ease of family entertaining sets just the right mood.

MENU

8 People

Bordeaux and Pouilly Fuissé

Fresh Crabmeat Canapés

* Christmas Duckling

* Wild Rice with Pecans

Turnip Puree   Braised Brussels Sprouts

*Romaine & Cucumber Salad with Oil &
Red Wine Vinegar*

*Basket of Hot Rolls (Caraway, Sesame
and Poppyseed)*

Coffee

* Down's Nesselrode Pudding

Rum Pumpkin Pie

SETTING THE STAGE

Your family deserves the best possible party. You want to treat yourselves as well as you'd treat guests—even better. But so often we don't put out the extra effort. This Christmas, make a glamorous feast using these few extra touches.

The Table

Props
red moiré silk cloth for table
white place plate per person
8-inch bough per person
small glass plate per person
silver platter
silver tray
3 pounds of kumquats with leaves attached
5 stems of holly

The vibrant red silk, the silver, and just a touch of special garnishes on the platters makes this table sparkle.

Setup
Cover table with red cloth.
Put place plate at each setting. Set small pine bough on table above place plate.
Serve crabmeat canapés on glass plate on top of place plate. Place on table before guests are seated.
Arrange duckling on large silver platter. Surround with kumquats. If not available, substitute a collar of watercress with two dozen lady apples sprinkled through it.
Place turnip puree in white or silver bowl. Set on large silver tray. Decorate tray with holly.

The Centerpiece

Props

round mirror or round of slate, 12 inches in
    diameter
silver cruet set with stand
silver gravy boat
silver salt and pepper set
silver creamer
5 red anemones
red amaryllis
6 small pink roses
8 red carnations
4 branches of holly (cut to 5 to 7 inches in
    length)

I'm always finding new ways to use common
serving pieces that are around the house. For
this party I love the elegance and surprise of
using odds and ends of silver to make a flower
arrangement. If you don't have a gravy boat, a
sugar bowl will do! Experiment with what you
have tucked away in your cupboards.

Setup

Place silver pieces on mirror or slate round.
Cut amaryllis to 10 inches. Place in cruet.
Put anemones in other cruet.
Place roses, carnations, and holly in remaining
    pieces.

COUNTDOWN

One Week Before
- ☐ Order duckling at least one week ahead of time.

Five Days Before
- ☐ Write out shopping list for decorations and groceries.

Four Days Before
- ☐ Buy nonperishable groceries and decorations.

Two Days Before
- ☐ Buy holly and pine boughs. Keep in water.

One Day Before
- ☐ Make rice stuffing. Refrigerate.
- ☐ Prepare Nesselrode pudding. Chill for at least six hours. Unmold. Refrigerate until served.
- ☐ Prepare pumpkin pie. Cover loosely with foil and let stand at room temperature until serving.
- ☐ Buy flowers.
- ☐ Make turnip puree. Reheat before serving.
- ☐ Prepare salad.

Party Day!
- ☐ Set table and arrange centerpiece.
- ☐ Begin cooking duckling 1½ to 2 hours before desired serving time.
- ☐ An hour before serving, prepare brussels sprouts.
- ☐ Prepare canapés in morning.

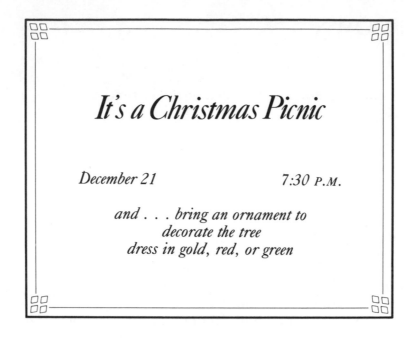

It's a Christmas Picnic

December 21   *7:30 P.M.*

*and . . . bring an ornament to
decorate the tree
dress in gold, red, or green*

*T*he perfect solution for holiday entertainment when you haven't much time, money, or room in your apartment is to get your pals together for the ultimate sit-down dinner—on the floor! It's the perfect way to share the holidays with those who are the dearest but who, on Christmas Day, will scatter and not be the nearest.

MENU

12 People

Gluhin—"Glowing Wine"

French Colombard

* Miniature Cheese Balls

Zucchini Boats with Julienne Vegetables

* Individual Chicken Curry Rice Casseroles

Escarole Salad with * Country French Dressing

French Rolls

Coffee

* Lemon Chess Tarts   Chocolate Truffles

Invitations

Send invitations written on a card attached to candy cane. Wrap candy cane in tissue paper and mail in stiff colored cardboard envelope. If you don't have enough floor pillows for everyone, include the request "please bring a pillow to sit on."

SETTING THE STAGE

The magic in this presentation comes in the bright red box of picnic food that every two guests share. They pick it up from the kitchen counter or buffet to take to the picnic area on the living room floor. This holiday party is a gift of love from you to your friends. What better way to show them than to gift wrap the meal, too? As an added touch, you can provide a stack of Christmas sheet music. Let your guests sing for their supper!

The Table

Props

quilt or red-and-white-checked tablecloth
floor pillows for seating
6 red, shiny Christmas present boxes, 12 by
    12 by 8 inches
12 sheets of red tissue paper
12 deep green or blue cloth napkins
12 covered onion soup pots
12 cupcake paper liners in pink or blue
    (depending on color of napkins)
12 half bottles of white wine
12 wine glasses
12 glass salad plates
12 small red or green shiny paper bags
glass salad bowl
red lacquer tray
12 red-and-white bows and name cards
large tambori table

Setup

Spread quilt or cloth on floor. Surround with
    floor pillows.
Cook curry in soup pots. Place lids on for
    serving.
Line each box with tissue paper.
Set 2 soup pots into center of box.
Wrap 2 sets of silverware up in cloth napkins
    and place in box.
Set half bottle of wine (opened and recorked)
    and two glasses into box.
Put 2 French rolls into each box.

Place individual lemon chess tarts and chocolate truffles in red or green paper bags. Put in box.

Close box and attach bow on top.

Arrange your "seating chart" by combining the two guests you think would like to share a meal and putting their names on the name card.

Place cheese balls in cupcake liners. Set on red lacquer tray alternating with zucchini boats filled with julienned carrots and celery. Set appetizers up on tambori table placed on edge of quilt or on coffee table.

Serve salad from glass bowl using glass plates. Set it out on coffee table next to quilt so guests can help themselves.

When guests unwrap their meals, have them place the box lids on the quilt as "placemats" for easier eating.

The Centerpiece

Props

12 white votive candles in glass holders
12-foot princess pine garland
12 red carnations
12 bud vials
large bunch holly

The Christmas picnic quilt is graced by flower-laced pine garlands to create a simple holiday centerpiece.

Setup

Place individual carnations into bud vials.

Weave pine garland across tabletop.

Insert vials into garland so they are completely covered. Place holly sprays in garland, around carnations.

COUNTDOWN

Three Weeks Before
- [ ] Mail invitations.

One Week Before
- [ ] Write out shopping list for decorations and groceries.

Five Days Before
- [ ] Begin to assemble serving pieces and decoration supplies.

Four Days Before
- [ ] Call guests who have not RSVP'd.

Three Days Before
- [ ] Finish assembling cooking and decoration supplies.
- [ ] Buy nonperishable groceries and centerpiece supplies.

Two Days Before
- [ ] Prepare dough for lemon chess tarts. Wrap in waxed paper and store in refrigerator.
- [ ] Make cheese balls. Store covered in refrigerator.
- [ ] Begin preparing chicken curry. Cook chicken, sauce, assemble. Reserve cheese.

One Day Before
- [ ] Finish curry. Top with cheese and bake. Store covered for reheating.
- [ ] Buy all perishable groceries. Buy flowers.
- [ ] Make salad dressing.

Party Day!
- [ ] Assemble party picnic boxes. Add chicken curry at last minute.
- [ ] Set up decorations and picnic cloth.
- [ ] Toss salad just before serving.

*You and me and the tree
makes three*

A Cozy Christmas Feast

just for us

7 P.M.

*T*he two of you—it's a chance for the most luscious of holiday indulgences. Embrace the quiet, celebrate the coziness. When you can make this day anything you want, what better than the dramatic elegance of the rarest delicacies for the palate? It's all part of your Christmas presents to one another.

MENU

2 People

Vodka with Lemon

Caviar   *Toast Rounds*

Caesar Salad

* Crab Mornay in Scallop Shells

* Artichoke Bottoms with Broccoli Puree

* Poached Pears with * Ginger Cream

Espresso

Crème de Cacao

SETTING THE STAGE

The beauty of this feast is in its dramatic simplicity and its portability. The trays can go from kitchen to coffee table or dining room with ease. A Christmas for two is reason to celebrate. Today families are scattered, and we often feel "Christmas isn't what it used to be." But there's no need to feel blue when the two of you can share such a special evening.

The vodka bottle, encased in a sleeve of holly-decorated ice, and caviar are a beautiful way to start this meal. Sip and nibble and wander into the kitchen together to set up the main course.

The Table

Props
round plastic juice pitcher
5 branches holly, 10 inches long
bottle vodka
shallow glass bowl, 8 inches in diameter
2 black or red lacquer trays
2 white scallop dishes, 5 inches in diameter
4 small Chinese lacquer soup bowls
2 Chinese porcelain salad plates
2 black cloth napkins
piece of lamé fabric to cover table

Setup

Drinks:
Boil a quart of water. Allow to cool to room
    temperature.
Fill juice pitcher half full.
Soak labels off vodka bottle. Place vodka
    bottle into center of pitcher so water comes
    up to the bottom of the neck.
Leave in freezer until water begins to freeze.
Take out pitcher and insert holly branches
    into slush around bottle. Return to freezer
    until ready to serve.
To remove bottle from ice, run warm water
    on outside of pitcher.
Place iced vodka bottle on glass bowl and
    bring to table.

Trays:
Set crab Mornay in shells on center of tray.
Serve artichokes in small bowls and salad on
   plates.
Tie napkin through handle on side of tray.

Dessert:
Serve pears in lacquered Chinese soup bowls.

The Centerpiece

Props

2 pots with single red amaryllis in each
package floral adhesive

2 bunches of galax leaves
5 votive candles on raised Chinese candle
   stands

A simple, striking candlelit centerpiece is all
that's required here. Put your favorite music
on the stereo, dim the lights, and relax.

Setup

Cover outside of clay pots with strips of floral
   adhesive.
Cover pots with galax leaves. Set pots on
   corner of table.
Put candles all around the table.

COUNTDOWN

One Week Before
- ☐ Write out shopping list for decorations and groceries.

Five Days Before
- ☐ Begin assembling decorations and serving supplies.

Four Days Before
- ☐ Buy nonperishable groceries.

Two Days Before
- ☐ Buy amaryllis

One Day Before
- ☐ Buy fresh food and vegetables.
- ☐ Put vodka in freezer to chill.

Party Day!
- ☐ Prepare ginger cream ahead of time.
- ☐ Prepare crab Mornay in the late morning. Reheat just before serving.
- ☐ Poach pears and chill four hours before serving.
- ☐ Prepare salad.
- ☐ Cook artichokes just before serving.

Holiday Open House

at Enid and Ralph's

December 28th   *4 P.M.*

Bring the whole family

RSVP

*T*he holiday season from early December through the first of January is a perfect time to have an open house for all your friends and family. Children, teenagers, grandparents, parents—all can come together at this party.

MENU

50–70 People

Eggnog

Chilled White Wine

Holiday Punch for Children

* Chicken Liver Pâté

Baked Brie

Ring of Cream Cheese with Minced Sweet Red Pepper

Melba Rounds & Baguette Slices

Tray of Smoked Fish (Whitefish, Salmon, Trout, Sable)

Mixed Green Salad with * Tahini Dressing (Alfalfa Sprouts, Escarole, Mushrooms, Beets, & Rings of Bermuda Onion)

Basket of Cranberry Bread or Muffins

* Warm Apple Raisin Pie

* Holiday Pumpkin Roll

Decorated Snowman Cookies

Hot Fruit Compote (Apricots, Prunes, Pears, & Nectarines)

Coffee with Kahlúa

Invitations

Send out a plain red card with a small sprig of pine and holly glued to the front. Glue pine to lower left corner angling up across the card. Put holly on top of pine and attach with glue. Paste a red stick-on seal over ends of holly and pine. Mail in oversized envelope.

SETTING THE STAGE

One of the great luxuries of this season is to combine the beauty of Christmas plants and greens with a few early blooming spring flowers that are available from greenhouses and special florists. The promise of what's to come and the pleasure of the current season join to set a very festive tone. Because this menu includes hearty hors d'oeuvres and luscious desserts, you'll want to set-up the food on a very long buffet that has ample room to separate the courses or use two smaller tables, one for each. If you use two tables, simply duplicate the centerpiece on both.

The Table

<u>Props</u>

Hors d'oeuvres:
white linen tablecloth
12-foot garland of princess pine
12 carnations: 6 red, 6 pink
12 bud vials

Desserts:
2 glass cake stands
large glass platter
large glass bowl
2 dozen candy canes
4 thick branches of myrtle, 8 inches long
package of cranberries

Drinks:
large glass punch bowl
round mirror, 14 inches in diameter
package angel hair
5 red carnations
5 bud vials
white tablecloth

The food is so colorful that the presentation on the serving platters is the way to establish the look on this table. Don't bring anything to the table that has not been garnished with greens (pine, watercress, myrtle, lemon leaves). Use plates that are glass or white.

Setup

Hors d'oeuvres:
Bring smoked fish, pâté, baked brie, and cream cheese to table on glass or white platters. Place on left side of buffet.
Take garland and wind it around each platter in a continuous "S" shape.
Put carnations into bud vials. Insert throughout garland.

Dessert:
Cover cake stands with bed of myrtle.
Put pumpkin roll (on glass plate) and apple raisin pie on top of myrtle beds.
Sprinkle fresh cranberries all through myrtle.
Cover glass platter with candy canes. Position them so the curved ends form a scalloped edge around the plate. Put cookies all over the bed of candy canes.
Serve fruit compote in large glass bowl.

Drinks:
Set punch bowl up on separate table, covered with a white cloth.
Place round mirror under bowl.
Cover mirror and base of bowl with angel hair.
Put carnations in bud vials and plant in angel hair around punch bowl. Make sure vials are completely covered.

The Centerpiece

The table is already decorated with all the special effort you've put into the food presentation, but one more touch—the beauty of flowers—makes it a completely finished table. If you can't find all the flowers I mention, use what is available as long as they are white, red, or pink. If flowers are out of the picture altogether, an alternative is to fill a hurricane glass and cylinder-shaped vases of various sizes with layers of rock candy, ribbon candy, and peppermints. You can cluster these together for a crystal and candy centerpiece.

Props

pot pink azaleas
2 pots red *kalanchoes*
pot white narcissus
4 pieces of green satin, 18 by 18 inches
4 pieces of green or red silk cord, 24 inches long

Pots of flowers do complete the table, but they can't be used with their clay or plastic containers showing. Wrapping them is easy and has a lot of impact.

Setup

Put each pot in the center of the satin square.

Draw cloth up, letting the fabric fold and crease naturally.

Tie up with silk cord as close to the top of the pot as possible.

Take fabric that remains above cord and fold over toward soil to form fluffy cuff that hides the top rim of the pot.

Place pots at back left-hand side of table behind hors d'oeuvres.

Set azalea in back, put the two red *kalanchoes* to the left, one slightly in front of the other. Set the narcissus to the right of the azalea.

COUNTDOWN

Three Weeks Before
- ☐ Mail invitations.

One Week Before
- ☐ Write out shopping list for decorations, groceries, and serving pieces.

Five Days Before
- ☐ Begin buying nonperishable groceries and decorations.

Four Days Before
- ☐ Call guests who have not RSVP'd.

Three Days Before
- ☐ Prepare chicken liver pâté.
- ☐ Buy potted plants.

Two Days Before
- ☐ Begin setting up basic decor and organizing serving dishes.

One Day Before
- ☐ Prepare pumpkin roll.
- ☐ Buy fresh flowers, vegetables, fruit, and smoked fish.

Party Day!
- ☐ Cook apple pie.
- ☐ Set up decorations in morning.
- ☐ Prepare salad dressing two hours ahead. Toss when ready to serve.

Sunny Southern Christmas

While the bitter winter winds blow across the north, visions of sugarplums melt under the warm southern sun. All the warmth and nostalgia of the season is felt in swimsuits as well as snowsuits, but the look and the feel of the holiday is different. It makes no sense to try to impose the look of a New England Christmas on an Arizona scene. The natural beauty of warm southern locales lends itself to very beautiful holiday decorating ideas.

Make your Christmas decorations work *with*, not against, the special look of a warm climate. The shell tree is a wonderful example of this technique (see p. 83). Wreaths made with fresh fruits—lemons, limes, clementines—and southern foliage, such as magnolia or banana leaves, are also lovely alternatives.

If your house is furnished with tropical garden print sofas and chairs, you may want to consider using plain pastel sheeting to slip-cover them to have a special look around holiday time.

Another modification from the traditional northern style of celebration can be made in the menu. In place of the heavy fare of baked yams, stuffing, and turkey, consider a menu that features grilled whole sea bass or flounder, or a Mexican feast with conch-lime seviche.

Let's bring in the New Year

*with a cozy dinner
together!*

*Evelyn and Leonard hope
you can come at 9:30 P.M.*

*December 31st to greet
the year and toast our friendship*

RSVP

Are the crowds and noise and hustle of New Year's Eve too much for you this year? What nicer solution than to plan a peaceful dinner with a few friends? This hearty but elegant menu lends itself to an evening spent at the table with good conversation, good company, and good cheer.

MENU

6 People

Champagne

Oysters on the Half Shell

*Stuffed Breast of Veal

*Potatoes Anna

Hot Buttered Asparagus

Italian Bread

Coffee

*Orange Rum Raisin Bombe

Shortbread Cookies

Cognac

Invitations

Send out art postcards of quiet rural French country scenes. Set the peaceful tone of the evening by avoiding splashy New Year's–style cards.

SETTING THE STAGE

Tonight you want to be a guest at your own celebration. What better way than to keep the setup simple but beautiful? The mushroom basket used here for the centerpiece is a year-round favorite of mine. You can find these long oval wooden baskets at any grocery that sells fresh mushrooms. Ask the grocer to save empty ones for you. I paint it pastel colors and fill it with pots of flowers in the spring and spray it gold for a breadbasket on a festive winter table.

The Table

<u>Props</u>
6 small ceramic ramekins
6 wooden place plates
paisley tablecloth
6 cream cloth napkins
6 10-inch glass plates
6 dark ceramic dinner plates
3 pounds of rock salt
chafing dish
large wicker basket, 6 by 12 inches tall

Throughout France tables are set with a rustic elegance that blends the practical with the refined. There is a simplicity and warmth to the look that is the perfect compliment to this dinner.

<u>Setup</u>
Cover table with cloth.
Set wooden place plates at each setting. Lay napkin across each place.
Arrange half a dozen raw oysters on mound of rock salt in glass plate.
Set on top of each place plate.
When oysters are eaten, remove plate. Bring out 6 ceramic plates for main course.
Put bread in tall wicker basket and set on table. Guests will tear off what they want.
Fill ramekins with individual portions of soft butter. Place above each knife.
Serve veal and asparagus from dark colored ceramic dishes. Serve potatoes Anna in chafing dish.

The Centerpiece

Props

natural colored mushroom basket
5 Peruvian lilies
5 bud vials
new potatoes, baking potatoes, and red
   potatoes—enough to fill basket ⅔ full
2 dozen large white mushrooms
8 stems of leather fern
5 brass candlesticks, various heights
5 white tapers

Blending in with the table setting, this small centerpiece is the perfect combination of the elegant and the natural.

Setup

Fill the mushroom basket with a combination
   of potatoes.
Make sure each type is clearly visible.
Top potatoes with a layer of mushrooms.
Cut lilies so that they vary from 4 to 10 inches
   long.
Place lilies in bud vials.
Sink vials into potato-mushroom arrangement
   so flowers seem to grow out of it.
Add short stems of leather fern around rim of
   basket.
Set at center of table with candlesticks to one
   side.

COUNTDOWN

Three Weeks Before
- [ ] Mail invitations.

One Week Before
- [ ] Order veal roast.

Five Days Before
- [ ] Write out shopping list for decorations and groceries.

Four Days Before
- [ ] Begin assembling decorations.
- [ ] Call guests who have not RSVP'd.

Three Days Before
- [ ] Buy nonperishable groceries.

One Day Before
- [ ] Prepare bombe. Freeze. Before serving, let sit at room temperature for 10 minutes.
- [ ] Combine marinade for veal. Baste meat and refrigerate overnight.
- [ ] Buy fresh flowers and vegetables.
- [ ] Get fresh oysters as late in day as possible. Do not open.

Party Day!
- [ ] Set table and arrangement in late afternoon.
- [ ] Put veal in oven two hours before desired serving time.
- [ ] Begin potatoes one hour before desired serving time.
- [ ] Open oysters and arrange on plates immediately before serving.

No matter who your team is . . .
team up with Tom and Kay

Super Bowl Sunday

2:30 P.M.

RSVP

*H*alf—that's right, half—the American population watches the Super Bowl every year! It's one great transcontinental party. So why not get your pals together and share the day? Even if you're not a fan, a Super Bowl Party is more fun than spending the day looking at the back of your spouse's head as you mutter about all the things you'd hoped to do together today.

MENU

12 People

Texas or Dos Equis Beer

* Chili con Queso with Tostada Chips

* Texas Chili with Condiments (Sour Cream, Scallions, Bacon Bits, Jalapeño Peppers)

Avocado Salad with Herb Dressing

Lemon Sherbet   Powdered Sugar Cookies

* Café Mexicano

Invitations

Send brightly colored striped cards or any post-cards you can find that have a football theme. If you want to go all out, find solid red bandanas like the referees use and write the invitation on them in black Magic Marker. Fold and mail in a brightly colored envelope.

SETTING THE STAGE

Bright colors, rough wood, ceramic, and fiery pepper plants set the look of this casual get-together. You might want to use your team's colors as your theme, or bring in pendants, pom-poms, and team emblems. If you do, repeat those colors in the tablecloth, paper plates, serving dishes, and flowers. For a more festive look, I've chosen to emphasize the Tex-Mex menu in my decorations.

The Table

Props

serapé or brightly striped tablecloth
red or yellow dishes
12 oversized cups for coffee
wreath of dried chili peppers
large glass bowl

You want to keep the setup simple and eye-catching. Guests will wander to the table off and on all afternoon. To keep the chili hot, you may serve it from a crock pot on the table or have it on the stove over a low flame.

Setup

Spread serapé on the diagonal over tabletop
Provide plastic plates with divided sections to
    keep food separate.
Pass the café Mexicano to guests as they
    watch the game.
Use the chili wreath—available at most
    Mexican or Chinese food stores—around
    the base of a glass bowl holding the chips.

The Centerpiece

Props

6 miniature cactus plants in clay pots
4 pots of red pepper plants
wreath of dried chili peppers
Jerusalem tomato plant, 8-inch-high pot with
    15-inch-tall plant

The colors of the peppers, tomatoes, and chili, and the texture of the cactus blend together to give this a fiery look. I have used this arrangement for an outdoor barbecue and for a summer cocktail party. With slight variations—the additions of zinnias and marigolds, the use of a red linen tablecloth, or one or two larger cacti—this basic setup can be used in many ways. Don't hesitate to experiment.

Setup

Put the pepper plants on one end of the table.

Surround with the miniature cacti. Use upside down clay pots, wooden stands, or mini tambori tables to elevate several of the cacti.

Place the tomato plant off to one side behind the peppers.

COUNTDOWN

Two Weeks Before
- ☐ Mail out invitations.

One Week Before
- ☐ Scout out centerpiece supplies and serapé (in foreign crafts store), or use tablecloth.

Five Days Before
- ☐ Check serving pieces and cookware. Buy or borrow what's needed.
- ☐ Write out shopping list for decorations and groceries.

Four Days Before
- ☐ Call guests who have not RSVP'd.
- ☐ Buy all nonperishable groceries.
- ☐ Buy potted pepper plants, cacti, chili wreath.

Three Days Before
- ☐ Prepare both chilis. Store in refrigerator in cooking pots.

Two Days Before
- ☐ Prepare salad dressing.
- ☐ Set up table and centerpiece.
- ☐ Set out all serving pieces.

Party Day!
- ☐ Prepare mixture for Mexican coffee. Refrigerate until you are ready to heat and serve.
- ☐ Heat chili and cheese sauce 15 minutes before serving. Prepare salad. Reserve dressing.
- ☐ Assemble nachos and heat just before guests arrive.
- ☐ Dress salad just before serving.

Have a Heart

Suzanne and Carlton

invite you and a friend
to an old fashioned Valentine's Day
Celebration

February 14   *7:30 P.M.*

Dessert Buffet
Dress Romantically

RSVP

*D*o you have enough nerve to throw an un-
abashedly sentimental celebration? You may
feel that friends will pooh-pooh such silliness,
but you'll be surprised at how much they'll
enjoy your romantic fantasy. So take it to the
limit with lace, hearts, and flowers. Valentine's Day is unquestionably one of the love-
liest holidays of the year.

MENU

20 People

Chenin Blanc

Champagne

Sauterne

* Coeur à la Crème with Fresh Raspberries

* Linzer Cookies

* Fresh Strawberry Tarts

* Gâteau au Chocolat

Tray of Fresh Melons and Grapes

Kenyan Coffee

Ceylon & Darjeeling Teas

Invitations

Send the funniest dime store Valentines as invitations. What else?

SETTING THE STAGE

It's wonderful to have an excuse to put on a really pretty, lacy party. When I was a child we used to make Valentine's cards from paper doilies and red construction paper and decorate them with candy hearts and violets. I've taken those memories and refined them to make this party just as delightful. I can't wait till next Valentine's Day to do this myself!

The Table

Props

2 wooden mushroom baskets, sprayed Chinese red
2 sheets each red, pink, and white tissue paper
silver cake stand
glass cake stand
4 large doilies
pink ceramic platter
pink felt tablecloth
overcloth of red tulle
3 boxes of tiny, red stick-on hearts
2 dozen tiny red silk or paper roses (dime store variety)
large bag of candy "I love you" hearts
large bag of red hot hearts
bunch baby's breath
2 dozen fresh strawberries

The tablecloth is the main attraction on the food table. Dishes, utensils, coffee service, and napkins are set out on a second small table or buffet adjacent to the food table. Cover this table with a pink felt undercloth and cover with white tulle.

Setup

Cover food table with felt. Lay tulle over it.

Dot the stick-on hearts all over the tulle.

Pin roses onto tulle in an all-over pattern.

Sprinkle red hot and candy hearts all over tabletop.

Set cake stands lined with doilies at center of table. Put chocolate cake on silver stand. Arrange strawberry tarts on glass stand.

Line red mushroom baskets with pink, red, and white tissue paper. Fill with Linzer cookies. Set baskets on two large overlapping doilies.

Place *coeur à la crème* on pink ceramic platter. Surround with fresh strawberries and baby's breath.

The Centerpiece

Props

silver tray

4 demitasse cups (mix or match patterns)

silver coffeepot

12 short stem, baby pink roses

3 bunches of baby's breath

6 red roses

This centerpiece is designed to blend in with the food presentation, not stand out from it. It is dainty, subtle, and very pretty.

Setup

Place demitasse cups on tray.

Fill each cup with roses and baby's breath.

Set coffeepot filled with roses to side of cup.

Set tray in back right-hand corner of the table.

COUNTDOWN

Two Weeks Before
- ☐ Mail invitations.

One Week Before
- ☐ Scout out centerpiece and tabletop supplies.

Five Days Before
- ☐ Spray mushroom baskets.
- ☐ Double check to see you have all cooking and serving pieces.

Four Days Before
- ☐ Call guests who have not RSVP'd.
- ☐ Write out shopping list for decorations and groceries.

Three Days Before
- ☐ Buy all nonperishable groceries.

Two Days Before
- ☐ Bake Linzer cookies. Store in airtight can.
- ☐ Buy all candies, remaining table and centerpiece supplies.
- ☐ Buy remaining groceries.

One Day Before
- ☐ Prepare *coeur à la crème* the evening before. Leave in mold. Cover and refrigerate.
- ☐ Prepare cream filling for strawberry tarts. Wash and drain strawberries and raspberries. Store filling and berries in refrigerator.
- ☐ Bake cake. Cool and store in tin at room temperature.
- ☐ Set up tablecloth and serving plates and dishes. Buy flowers.

Party Day!
- ☐ Arrange flowers. Put finishing touches on table.
- ☐ 2 hours before serving, unmold *coeur à la crème*. Let sit in refrigerator. Top with raspberries just before serving.
- ☐ Immediately before serving, assemble strawberry tarts.

PERSONAL PARTY CALENDAR

Chapter Eight
PERSONAL PARTIES

*T*he yearly cycle of celebration is not limited just to calendar holidays! Fill your life with special occasions that are private, personal statements of how you feel. Echo the ebb and flow of your moods and fortunes. Share your feelings with your friends and family.

While I love the celebrations that dot the yearly calendar, the most special parties are those that you give when you have something unique and personal to rejoice in! The parties that follow celebrate everything from birthdays to showers, weddings to anniversaries. Now, these are personal parties that we

all can anticipate from year to year. One goal should be to try and add surprising personal parties, too. For example, you may want to fête your friend when he or she gets a new job, or throw a housewarming party for someone who has just moved. These very specific parties are a direct expression of your interest and concern with the events of your friends' lives and let you make a grand expression of your feelings! There is no occasion that can't be the spark for a fabulous party. Caring for yourself and your loved ones—that's the real key to personal parties!

It's a

Ho-Hum Birthday

Thursday, November 23

for my 33rd year
come share some cheer

no gifts more than $1.98

dinner at 8

RSVP

*F*or those off-year birthdays, this party can't be beat. You are the host at your own birthday party. Celebrate yourself! There is no reason to be alone or feel forgotten on this important day. If you feel funny about soliciting gifts tell your friends, "No gifts." Or if you'd like to see what silly ideas they come up with, limit them to $1.98!

MENU

6–8 guests

Sake   Cuovo Wine

* Beef Scallion Rolls

* Cold Shrimp with Soy-Mustard Sauce

* Pasta Primavera

* Oriental Bean Sprout Salad

Lichee Nuts   * Babas au Rhum

Espresso

Invitations

Make your own invitations out of rice paper squares decorated with colorful stick-on hearts, stars, or any other picture you like.

SETTING THE STAGE

The Chinese invented pasta and the Italians perfected it! So it is not really surprising that Oriental and Italian food blend so well together. For this ho-hum birthday, I've chosen my favorite foods, and you should do the same. Remember, this is your day!

The decorations for this celebration are a blend of simple lacquered bowls and handsome Italian and Japanese bamboo and wicker accessories.

The Table

<u>Props</u>

2 tatami mats, 2 by 3 feet for tablecloth
2 paper fans, approx. 12-inches across when opened
8 black lacquer plates
8 small black rice bowls
8 small bowls for mustard-soy sauce
wicker bread basket
8 lacquer or wicker place trays
8 black dinner plates
chopsticks and flatware at each setting

This is a seated dinner. You want to set the appetizers on the table when your guests are seated. After that, you can clear off the lacquer plates, bring in the white dinner plates, pasta, and salad.

<u>Setup</u>

Cover table with tatami mats.
Place one tray at each place setting.
Set black lacquer plate in tray. Put small sauce bowl next to plate. Rest chopsticks across top of plate. Place rice bowls on plate to hold bean sprout salad.
Arrange beef scallion rolls lengthwise along one of the fans. Place shrimps, several to a toothpick, along the second fan. Set on table.

The Centerpiece

Props

2 bonzai trees
18-inch circle of slate
2 cupfuls of black pebbles
6 mini bud vases, Oriental style
6 sprigs of greenery and/or flowers
4 votive candles and holders

A simple, delicate Oriental arrangement placed on the slate adds to the whimsy of this meal.

Setup

Place bonzai trees on slate round.
Put greenery in bud vases.
Surround slate round with pebbles. Make a small "path" leading to the opposite corner of the slate.
Set candles and bud vases alongside path.

COUNTDOWN

Two Weeks Before
- ☐ Mail invitations.

One Week Before
- ☐ Write out shopping list for decorations, groceries, and serving pieces.
- ☐ Begin assembling serving pieces.

Four Days Before
- ☐ Call guests who have not RSVP'd.
- ☐ Buy all nonperishable groceries.
- ☐ Buy bonzai trees and centerpiece supplies.

One Day Before
- ☐ Marinate beef.
- ☐ Set up table and centerpiece.
- ☐ Bake babas.

Party Day!
- ☐ In morning, assemble pasta primavera. Refrigerate.
- ☐ Prepare and refrigerate salad three hours before serving.
- ☐ Marinate shrimp for 3 to 4 hours. Skewer and allow to come to room temperature before serving.
- ☐ Broil beef.
- ☐ Assemble beef scallion rolls.
- ☐ Cook pasta sauce several hours early and refrigerate. Add to pasta before serving.

Bobbie's Fifth Birthday

May 21st   *12 to 2 P.M.*

Come in playclothes

RSVP

*C*hildren's birthdays are very special, but they can be draining. My rule of thumb is to have only as many guests as the child's age. Keep the party short, activity-filled and, if possible, contained in one child-proof room (the child's bedroom or a den, for example). For kids this young there is no need to splurge on extravagant favors or activities. Let them use their imaginations and do things for themselves.

MENU

6 Friends

Natural Fruit Punch

Mini Franks and Burgers

Potato Chips

Individual Bundles of Trail Mix

Decorated Cupcakes

Push Up Ice Cream Sticks

Invitations

Choose paper invitations with pictures of your child's favorite cartoon character. Or buy puzzle invitations, which have to be assembled by the children to find out the information.

SETTING THE STAGE

The setup for this party should concentrate on the special touches, for that's how you entertain the kids and keep them from getting restless and fussy. The table and centerpiece can be decorated, if you choose, by using your child's favorite cartoon character—Snoopy, R2D2, or Cookie Monster, for example—but simple paper plates and a paper cloth of any kind will do as well. I think the excitement and fantasy comes alive for kids when they get to play an active role in the party. Five-year-olds are too young to sit quietly and be entertained by movies, a clown, or a puppet show.

Special Touches

Set out long rolls of brown wrapping paper along the walls of the party room. Provide boxes full of crayons and let the kids draw a super mural! In one area of the room, set out large cardboard cartons with doors and windows cut in them. You may want to decorate one large box—as a castle or space ship—to get the idea across. Then have the kids decorate the others and make a mini-city or rocket that they can crawl in and out of. Serve their food in individual tin beach pails. Tie helium balloons to bucket handles. Place paper hats and noisemakers on the table. Sparklers for the cake add extra excitement. Don't forget to take Polaroid pictures of the party.

COUNTDOWN

Two Weeks Before
- [ ] Mail invitations.

Four Days Before
- [ ] Write out shopping list for decorations and groceries.
- [ ] Begin to assemble props for decorations.

Three Days Before
- [ ] Call guests who have not RSVP'd.

Two Days Before
- [ ] Assemble packages of trail mix.
- [ ] Buy nonperishable groceries.

One Day Before
- [ ] Set-up cardboard carton arrangement.
- [ ] Bake cupcakes.

Party Day!
- [ ] Set-up decorations and eating areas.
- [ ] Prepare rest of food.

Sweet Sixteen

It's a makeup–sleep over

Lauren's 16th birthday party

5 P.M.   *Saturday, August 13th*

Bring a sleeping bag and
a favorite record

RSVP

*S*weet sixteen is not as sweet these days as it was in my day! But if you want to find a balance between being modern and being traditional, consider this all-girls slumber party for your young lady. Arrange for a makeup consultant to come to your house for a demonstration. You can arrange to buy one lipstick for each girl. If they want any additional items, they're on their own.

MENU

6 People

"Make Your Own Pizzas"

* Pizza Dough

* Tomato Sauce

*Pizza Toppings (Mozzarella Cheese,
Pepperoni, and Mushrooms)*

Tossed Salad

Cola, Ginger Ale, Fruit Juice

* Ice Cream Delight Birthday Cake

Hot Fudge and Caramel Sauces

Invitations

Send funny pop art cards or pretty lacy ones—
whatever suits your daughter's personality.
The important thing to remember here is to
clue the guests into the fact that this is a
makeup party. Also indicate if they should
bring sleeping bags.

SETTING THE STAGE

You will need to set-up both the demonstration area and the dining area. To simplify this
task, you can use snack tables for both. When
the demonstration is over, the area can be
cleared for eating. Then all you have to do is
set out the pizza fixings and the guests can
help themselves.

The Table

Props

bright green tablecloth
2 wooden pizza paddles with handles
6 wooden salad bowls, to hold toppings
wooden salad bowl
multi-colored paper napkins and paper plates

The pizza paddles are available commercially,
but you might try renting or borrowing them
from a local pizzeria. They look wonderful and
are very practical, too. If you can't find them, I
suggest you use wooden cutting boards or
plywood rounds instead.

Setup

Cover table with cloth.
Set hot pizza on boards and bring to table.
Place condiments in semicircle near pizza.
Have salad service near paper plates and
    napkins.
Relax, the kids can help themselves!

The Centerpiece

Props

16 white candles of various sizes
16 cut flowers of various types, all in shades
    of white or pink
16 bud vases
20 lengths of colored ribbons, 5 feet long
    (pink or white, both solid and patterned)

Using a combination of 16 candles and flowers you can create a centerpiece that is feminine, pretty, and not too fussy. When combining the flowers, remember to vary heights on the table. I love to put the flowers in bird's nest baskets.

Setup

Weave ribbons on a diagonal across the table-top.

Place candles and flowers in an asymmetrical pattern along the length of the ribbons.

For an added touch, sprinkle paper rose petals between candles and flowers.

Special Touches

To set-up the demonstration area, place 6 snack tables in a semicircle in front of the card table the beauty consultant will be using for her show.

Drape each table with a white terry towel.

Place a mirror on each table. If possible, supply some lighted makeup mirrors. Provide several wicker baskets filled with brushes, combs, hair driers, makeup remover, creams, and various accessories such as emery boards, tweezers, eyelash curlers, etc.

Have a good supply of women's and fashion magazines around.

When the demonstration is over, clear off the snack tables. Drape with checkered napkins. The girls can then dine from the same tables.

COUNTDOWN

Two Weeks Before
- ☐ Mail invitations.
- ☐ Contact makeup consultant for demonstration.

One Week Before
- ☐ Write out shopping list for decorations and groceries.

Five Days Before
- ☐ Assemble props and buy nonperishable groceries.

Four Days Before
- ☐ Call guests who have not RSVP'd.

Three Days Before
- ☐ Make ice cream cake. Freeze until time to serve.

Two Days Before
- ☐ Make ribbon "cloth" for centerpiece.
- ☐ Make tomato sauce. Refrigerate.

One Day Before
- ☐ Buy flowers and fresh vegetables.
- ☐ Make pizza dough. Refrigerate.

Party Day!
- ☐ Set up demonstration area and food table.

*The First and
the Finest Anniversary*

*F*riends or family may choose to wine and dine you on your first anniversary, but let them do it the weekend before or after. Save that special night just for the two of you.

This romantic interlude doesn't have to be reserved for your first anniversary. Any time you and your special loved one want to take time to steal away for a fantasy evening, try this magic celebration. The key is to indulge yourself in simple elegant pleasures, fine food, good wine, and cozy company.

MENU

Champagne

Cold Marinated Sea Scallops en Brochette

French Bread

Explorateur Cheese

Fresh Raspberries with Crème Fraiche

Silvered Almonds

Espresso

SETTING THE STAGE

You want to transform your bedroom and bath into a salon for dining and dwelling. All surfaces should be cleared of clutter and knick-knacks. Lots of pillows, a fluffy new bed cover, fresh terry cloth robes, and oodles of candlelight and flowers will make this a memorable evening.

The Table

Props

3 snack trays
4 stems of small bloom orchids
3 linen and lace cloths to cover them
silver champagne bucket
large bunch of lemon leaves
your best china and silver: platters for cheese and bread; bowls for scallops and dessert
doilies

Simple and elegant, this setup is designed to go at your bedside.

Setup

Place snack trays along one side of the bed.
Cover with cloths.
Set bread, cheese, and fruit on one table.
Decorate all platters with doilies.
Garnish with flowers and leaves.
Arrange scallops on dinner plates and set on remaining snack trays.
Place chocolate truffles in a glass candy dish and set on bedside table.

The Centerpiece

Props

artichoke bloom
anthurium
2 bird of paradise flowers
4 cymbidium orchids
a bounty of candles
large 18-inch vase
18-inch red silk cord

This is the basic arrangement. You can expand it as much as you like. The look and feel is sumptuous and jungly. Additional flowers by the bed, on the dresser, and garnishing all the food will only increase the romantic feeling!

Setup

Place candles all around. No electric lights at
all tonight!

Arrange the flowers in a large urn-shaped vase
at least 18 inches tall. Tie a red silk cord
around the neck of the vase. Place up high
so that the impact of the flowers is
increased.

Special Touches

I would end this meal with dessert in a steamy
bubble bath for two! Transport the champagne, raspberries, and you to the tub. Place a
snack tray by the bath to hold the food. Fill the
room with candlelight and have two terry robes
for you to don after you have soaked and
sipped!

◇————————————◇

COUNTDOWN

Three Days Before
- [ ] Make sure you have the decorations, serving pieces, bed linens, and bubble bath.

Two Days Before
- [ ] Write out shopping list for decorations and groceries. If necessary, order scallops.

One Day Before
- [ ] Buy and arrange flowers.

Party Day!
- [ ] Buy bread and fresh fruit.
- [ ] Marinate and assemble scallops.
- [ ] Set cheese out to reach room temperature one hour before serving.
- [ ] Chill champagne in ice 30 minutes before serving.

Moving In!

*Let's Have a Party
in my new apartment*

August 13   7 P.M.

dress for sawdust!
RSVP

---

*B*are floors, packing boxes, and not a picture on the walls but it's home now, and what better way to settle in than to surround yourself with your friends for a super takeout feast? This is personal celebrating at its very essence. I believe it is the spirit and the people that are the most important part of any get-together. Decor, food, and presentation are an expression of those inner feelings, not a substitute for them. So don't be bashful about having guests over when you are not yet all set-up!

MENU

8-10 guests

6' Hero Sandwich

(cold cuts, cheeses, lettuce, tomato, and dressings)

Chips (potato, corn, tortilla)

Deli Salads (cole slaw, macaroni, 3 bean, and marinated cucumber)

Chocolate chip cookies

Fresh fruit bowl

Sangria   *Beer*

Invitations

Use brown wrapping paper and brightly colored inks to create your own invitations. Whatever you do, make sure you alert your guests to dress for casual fun. And they may need to "work" for their dinner!

SETTING THE STAGE

When you don't have any furniture, you can still create a buffet and table setup by using what's around. A sawhorse table, a picnic cloth drawn onto sheets of brown wrapping paper, and instant lighting with uplight behind the parasols will do the trick.

The Table

Props

2 sawhorses
plywood board, 3 by 5 feet
large roll of brown wrapping paper, 3 feet wide
parasol, 4 to 6 feet in diameter
2 uplights
2 paint roller pans
painter's hats

Keep with the look of the house by using painting supplies as serving dishes. You can improvise here, combining paper plates, available dishes, and some of the suggestions explained below.

Setup

Make a buffet table out of the sawhorses and plywood.
Cover with a length of brown paper.
Use two spanking clean paint rolling pans to hold the deli salads. Put the chips into the painter's hats.
Place parasol on one end of the table with spot behind it. This provides lighting that is gentle and looks very pretty.

The Centerpiece

Props

1 length of brown paper 3 by 12 feet
crayons
floor cushions
Brown luncheon bags with sand and candles
  in the bottom

Your "dining table" is a centerpiece all by it-self. Since you decorate it and make a colorful "arrangement" right on the wrapping paper, you can create any kind of setting you like.

Set Up

Make a table using the wrapping paper.
Using the crayons, draw on place mats, plates, silverware, glasses, and napkins.
At the center of the table draw an arrangement of funny flowers in a big basket. Keep colors clear and vivid!
For an extra touch, create a three dimensional arrangement of rollers and paint brushes with yardstick, scissors, and hammer in a vase, and place it to one end of the "table."
Consider using a houseplant, such as a ficus tree, next to the buffet to add a touch of green.

◇————————————————◇

COUNTDOWN

Two Weeks Before
- ☐ Mail invitations.

Three Days Before
- ☐ Get table setting supplies—wrapping paper, parasol, etc.

Two Days Before
- ☐ Contact takeout food shop and arrange for menu.

Party Day!
- ☐ Draw the "table." Arrange the sawhorse table.
- ☐ Have food delivered. Set up just before serving.

> *Joanna's Gotten Her*
>
> # Slice of the Pie
>
> *so let's*
> *share it with her*
> *on*
>
> April 12th   9:30 P.M.
>
> *at Beverly's*
> RSVP

When your best friend has a success—she passes the bar, gets a promotion, is elected president of her club—honor her with a slice-of-the-pie party.

There is a special feeling that comes with making an occasion like this to fête a friend. Parties are a chance to express our affections in many ways, and as a gift of love it is an occasion that you and your guest of honor will long remember.

MENU

8 People

Lattice Top Apple Pie with Vermont Cheddar Cheese

* Boston Cream Pie

* Chocolate Rum Pie

Coffee Bar

Garnishes
(Shaved Chocolate, Cinnamon Sticks, Lemon Zest, and Fresh Whipped Cream)

Liqueurs
(Kahlúa, Sambuca, Amaretto)

Invitations

Fold a sheet of colored construction paper in half. Cut a wedge-shaped triangle so that the top of the piece of pie (where the "crust" would be) is on the fold. Then use crayons to color on the crust. Inside, pen the information in brightly colored magic marker.

SETTING THE STAGE

To celebrate a success, set a mood of glitter and gold using an array of glass beads, gold foil, rhinestones, and sequins. There is something particularly sumptuous about an all-dessert party anyway, since it indulges our favorite food vice—rich, sweet, satisfying taste treats.

The Table

Props

gold lamé tablecloth
3 hat boxes
3 glass cake stands
a bounty of red and white or flowered tissue
 paper
8 white place plates
8 red and gold or black dessert plates

The look here is of the pies emerging from decorated hat boxes—like wonderful presents. The lamé cloth can be a remnant bought at any fabric store.

Setup

Cover table with lamé cloth.
Fill each hat box with a nest of tissue paper.
Set cake stands into boxes. They should
 come just to the top of the sides.
Top with the individual pies.
Serve the pie on dessert plates set on top of
 larger place plates. This makes for much
 easier handling, and guests don't have to
 worry about getting crumbs on themselves
 or the furniture.

The Centerpiece

Props

4 glass bowls, 8 inches in diameter
fake pearls, gold sequins, gold-covered
    chocolate coins, "diamond" rhinestones
4 red camelias
4 bud vases

Placed across the tabletop, these arrangements
pave the table with gold!

Setup

Fill each bowl full of either pearls, gold coins,
    gold sequins, or "diamond" rhinestones.
Place each flower in a bud vase and insert into
    center of glass bowl.
Place on table around hat boxes.
Sprinkle table with remaining pearls, etc., to
    spread the glitter.

COUNTDOWN

Two Weeks Before
- ☐ Mail invitations.

One Week Before
- ☐ Write out shopping list for decorations and groceries.

Five Days Before
- ☐ Begin assembling props for decorations.

Four Days Before
- ☐ Buy nonperishable groceries.
- ☐ Call guests who have not RSVP'd.

One Day Before
- ☐ Buy fresh flowers and remaining groceries.
- ☐ Make components for Boston cream pie. Store separately.

Party Day!
- ☐ Set-up decorations and set table.
- ☐ Make chocolate rum pie.
- ☐ Assemble Boston cream pie.
- ☐ Make or buy apple pie.

Wedding Shower

for

Ann and Jim

Sunday, May 12   *2:30 P.M.*

*Bring a copy of your
favorite mail-order catalog
for the bride and groom to select gifts from*

RSVP

MENU

20 People

Chilled White Wine

Bloody Marys

* Shrimp Aurore in Puff Pastry Shells

Herbed Long Grain Rice

Hot Buttered Carrots

Chilled Tomatoes with Fresh Basil

Miniature Rolls & Corn Muffins
Sweet Butter

Coffee

* Amaretto Ice Cream Pie

Invitations

Plain or fancy any standard shower invitation will do. Be sure to provide the information about this special variation however: your guests will each bring a mail-order catalog, and the bridal couple will have a chance to shop for gifts and let their friends know just what they need or want. I recommend setting a price limit—say $50 per gift. Several friends can pool together to buy one gift or to get a more expensive item if they choose. There is no need for you to decide on gifts while the bridal couple is there, just collect all the information. It's the perfect way to make sure that every gift hits the mark!

SETTING THE STAGE

These decorations blend the romantic feel of a wedding with the casual spirit of a cocktail buffet.

The Table

<u>Props</u>
20 wicker paper plate holders
5 snack tables
full length batik tablecloth for buffet
5 small batik cloths for snack tables
5 bud vases
10 flowers

At a buffet party like this, you want to provide some snack tables for guests to use to rest their glasses, ashtrays, salt and pepper shakers, and plates. Since everyone is seated casually around the living room on sofas and chairs, the snack tables are simply an addition to coffee and end tables.

Setup

Drape buffet with batik cloth.

Set out plates in wicker plate holders so that eating off the knees is not too tricky!

Drape snack tables with cloths and set strategically around the living room.

Set salt and pepper on trays, along with ashtrays and small bud vases with flowers, (cornflowers and yellow lilies, for example).

The Centerpiece

Props

3 wicker baskets of various sizes
collection of various kitchen supplies, garden tools, and bath accessories
3 batik scarves

This centerpiece is a gift from the host/hostess to the bridal couple. It provides a lovely sampling of some of the household objects they will need and provides a souvenir of the shower, too.

Setup

Line the three baskets with the batik scarves so they spill over the rims.

Fill each basket with an array of items. One basket could have an egg beater, a timer, wooden spoons, a rolling pin, dish towels; another could have flower seeds, a hoe and trowel, plant scissors, oasis; the last could contain bubble bath, soaps, potpourri, creams, shampoos, etc.

Place the baskets on the buffet table. Include a card so they know the baskets are a present.

Special Touches

This is a catalog party! When guests arrive with their favorites, have them stack them in a pretty white wicker basket festooned with ribbons. You should supply some additional catalogs, too, such as L.L. Bean, Conran's, Williams Sonoma, Spiegel.

After the lunch, bring out the catalogs and let everyone go through them. Provide the couple with bright red Magic Markers so they can circle their choices. After the party, the host can collect the information from each catalog and write out a Master list for the guests to use as a shopping guide.

◇————————————————◇

COUNTDOWN

Three Weeks Before
- ☐ Mail invitations.

One Week Before
- ☐ Write out shopping lists for decorations and groceries.

Five Days Before
- ☐ Begin assembling centerpiece props.

Four Days Before
- ☐ Buy nonperishable groceries.
- ☐ Call guests who have not RSVP'd.

Three Days Before
- ☐ Prepare Amaretto ice cream pies. Freeze.

One Day Before
- ☐ Make Bloody Mary mix.
- ☐ Buy fresh vegetables and shrimp.

Party Day!
- ☐ Prepare salad in morning. Pour over dressing just before serving.
- ☐ Make shrimp mixture early in day. Refrigerate. Add to pastry shells and heat just before serving.
- ☐ Set up tables and buffet.
- ☐ Cook vegetables one hour before meal. Reheat just before serving.

> ## Shower Susan
>
> *with*
>
> *GOOD WISHES*
>
> *for her baby*
>
> *1 P.M.*
>
> *at Judy's house*
> *hosted by*
> *Judy and Mary*
>
> *RSVP*

*T*his baby shower is a ladies' lunch. And it has a new twist. In addition to giving gifts, you might give a service. Each person writes out her pledge—to feed the cat during vacation, to plant a flower garden, to give a weekly manicure for two months, to form a baby-sitting pool, to make baby clothes, to do something that draws on their talents. It's a very personal expression of love and good wishes.

MENU

Luncheon

20–25 Ladies

White Wine Spritzers

Cream of Watercress Soup (hot or chilled)

** Spinach & Cheese Quiche
Ham & Mushroom Quiche*

Broccoli Salad with Lemon Vinaigrette

Hot Brioches   *Sweet Butter*

Iced Tea

Coffee

** Crispy Meringue Shells with Sugared
Peaches*

Invitations

I see the most delicate, lacy, candy-colored invitations here, or else make your own by folding colored paper into a diaper secured with a diaper pin! All the information is written inside, and the card must be unfolded to find it!

SETTING THE STAGE

No need to hold back on a sentimental occasion like this. Let all things feminine and childlike prevail! The table should be all white from the cloth to the dishes. Delicate pink roses, charming dollhouse furniture and, if possible, an old-fashioned wicker baby or doll carriage completes the look.

The Table

Props

blue tablecloth
pink serving bowl
2 large pink platters
2 large white paper doilies
pink and blue linen napkins
pink and blue ribbons
20 to 25 1½-inch-long baby dolls

Using the traditional baby colors of pink and blue, you can set a table that is both pretty and whimsical.

Setup

Cover buffet table with cloth.
Arrange broccoli salad in pink serving dish.
Set quiches on large pink platters lined with doilies.
Tie napkins around flatwear with length of ribbon.
Slip one baby doll under each ribbon.

The Centerpiece

Props

doll house furniture: chairs, sofas, etc.
15 1- to 2-inch baby dolls
4 pacifiers
2 baby rattles
cardboard tube, 6 inches long
12 large cloth diapers
large lace doily
bunch baby's breath
bunch violets
12-inch clay pot, sprayed white, filled with
    Styrofoam
bud vials
15 feet of satin ribbon, ½ inch wide
24-inch paper parasol in a solid pastel color
baby carriage
baby quilt

Setup

Spray clay pot white. Fill with Styrofoam.
Insert parasol handle into pot. Secure.
Tie a satin ribbon to each parasol spoke.
    Attach baby doll to each ribbon. Make sure
    they hang at various lengths.
Place parasol on buffet just right of center.
To make diaper "cake": Wind diapers
    continuously around center tube. Secure
    with straight pins. When last diaper is on,
    pin securely with diaper pins.
Decorate top with pacifiers and rattles.
Put "cake" on doily-lined platter.
Sprinkle doll house furniture down length of
    table.
Place baby carriage to side of buffet table.
    Line with quilt.
Make an album of all the guests pledges of
    service. Place in carriage along with other
    presents.

COUNTDOWN

Two Weeks Before
- ☐ Mail invitations.

One Week Before
- ☐ Write out shopping list for decorations and groceries.

Five Days Before
- ☐ Begin assembling serving pieces and props.

Four Days Before
- ☐ Call guests who have not RSVP'd.
- ☐ Make diaper "cake."

Three Days Before
- ☐ Gather service pledges from guests and assemble album.

Two Days Before
- ☐ Make meringue shells. Store in airtight container.
- ☐ Assemble parasol for centerpiece.

One Day Before
- ☐ Prepare watercress soup. Refrigerate.
- ☐ Set-up buffet and centerpiece.
- ☐ Buy flowers, peaches, and vegetables.

Party Day!
- ☐ Cut and sugar peaches in the morning.
- ☐ Fill shells just before serving.
- ☐ Cook broccoli early in day. Add marinade and refrigerate until time to serve.
- ☐ Prepare quiche filling and pastry crust early in the day. Finish quiches 1 hour before serving.

> *Come Share Our Joy at the*
>
> ## *Marriage of Our Daughter*
>
> *June 10th,*
>
> *Tea/Reception*   *4–7 P.M.*
>
> *R.SVP*

*T*he splendor and beauty of a spring or summer wedding outdoors at your home blends perfectly with the joy of the occasion. This tea/reception for up to 200 is a magnificent affair spread out under a tent, complete with a dining area and dance floor. The set up, logistics, and decorations are not only for weddings, however. Whenever your calendar calls for a really extravagant entertainment, this party can serve as a model. Don't hesitate to try it!

MENU

200 People

* *Champagne Punch*

Tea

Coffee

* *Hot Cheese Puffs*

Tea Sandwiches
(Watercress, Cucumber, Shrimp, Chicken
Salad)

Tray of Pastries
(Napoleons, Baklava, Eclairs, Palmiers,
Fresh Fruit Tarts)

Trays of Cookies
(Russian Tea Cookies, * Mexican Wedding
Cookies, Miniature Fruit Cakes, Triple
Layer Brownies)

Wedding Cake

Chocolate Wafer Mints   Rock Candy

Invitations

Wedding invitations are very much a matter of personal taste. If you are having yours engraved, I suggest a creamy white card with black ink or a card trimmed in a delicate pink border with black ink.

SETTING THE STAGE

Your role in setting up this party is to be the supervisor and planner. You will be working with a caterer, florist, the tent company, musicians, and a whole roster of workers. You must have a definite idea of what you want before you approach any of them or you will not be able to evaluate their advice or help them create the look that you want. Let's look at each component, step by step.

Tent Setup

200 guests, buffet service with music and
    dancing
Tent dimensions: 3750 square feet
20 tables, each seating 10 people
buffet area
dance floor and four-piece band (takes up area
    24 by 28 feet) or dance floor and eight-
    piece band (takes up area 24 by 32 feet)

The Tent Decorations

Props

2 spotlights with pink bulbs
2 pieces of pink tulle, 54 inches wide by 3
    yards long
2 40-foot garlands of green leaves
pink camelias, rubrum lilies, heather,
    gardenias
bud vials

A tent this size has two center poles. Incorporate them into the overall decor by dressing them in a bounty of blooms.

Setup

Place spotlights at top of tent poles, pointing
    up. Use pink bulbs.
Wrap poles in pink tulle.
Run garlands around the length of the poles
    on top of tulle.
Insert flower buds in water-filled vials and
    wire these into the garlands so they are
    studded with blooms.

The Buffet Table

Props

Ionic column, 5 feet tall
Corinthian column, 3 feet tall
Doric column, 3 feet tall
3 white, urn-shaped vases, 30 inches tall
baby's breath, heather, camelias, gardenias,
   rubrum lilies, white stock, white quince,
   calla lilies, pink snapdragons, blue
   delphinium, lavender larkspur
tulle (white or palest pink)
pale mint-green linen buffet cloth
length of white dotted swiss to cover buffet
15 foot buffet table

By continuing the delicate look of tulle and
flowers begun with the tent poles and adding
the drama of Greek columns, this buffet becomes a magnificent backdrop for the whole
party.

Setup

Cover buffet with linen and dotted swiss.
Set columns up along the back of buffet, 3
   feet apart.
Place vases filled with flowers on the
   columns. Place tallest column in center.
   Flank with 3-foot columns.
Wrap flowers with tulle. Secure with hat pin.

Buffet Food Presentation

Props

silver service
silver coffee samovar
silver tea service
tulle (white or palest pink)
camelias
green garlands
column tops, approximately 8 to 18 inches
   high

Renting silver service pieces for the day is a wonderful additional touch to really make this table sparkle. Using column tops as "tables" for food platters, draping them with tulle, and surrounding the sandwiches and desserts with blooms unifies the look.

Setup

Place column tops across buffet. Swath in tulle.

Arrange tea sandwiches, cheese puffs, and desserts on silver platters.

Garnish with flowers.

Set platters on column tops.

Wind garlands over table from column to column.

Individual Tables

Props

white linen tablecloths

white dotted swiss cloths long enough to cover table and touch floor

round glass vase, 8 inches high

baby's breath, heather, gardenias, camelias, rubrum lilies

silver place plate per setting

linen napkins in hues of pink, lavender, melon, magenta

A mini-version of the large floral arrangements decorates the center of each table. The gossamer cloths and silver place plates add a finishing touch.

Setup

Cover table with dotted swiss cloths.
Arrange flowers in each glass vase.
Set out 10 place plates per table.

Additional Touches

Props

4 6-foot Greek columns
4 white vases, 30 inches tall
an abundance of tulle (white or palest pink)
peonies, dogwood, iris, stock, snapdragons
garlands

Placed in four areas of the tent, this final arrangement completes the decor.

Setup

Arrange flowers in vases and swath in tulle as
  before.
Place on columns. Drape columns with
  garlands.

COUNTDOWN

Two Months Before
- ☐ Draw up guest list. Mail invitations.
- ☐ Contact tent rental company.
- ☐ Contact, compare, and try out caterers.

One Month Before
- ☐ Finalize and review decorations with chosen caterer.
- ☐ Contract for musicians.

Two Weeks Before
- ☐ Sample caterer's menu, make adjustments.

One Week Before
- ☐ Keep in touch with all suppliers to make sure they are proceeding correctly.

Two Days Before
- ☐ Have tent erected.
- ☐ Have chairs and tables delivered.
- ☐ Bring in electricians; test sound system.

One Day Before
- ☐ Assemble all props.
- ☐ Have caterer set-up kitchen as needed.
- ☐ Have band arrive for sound check.

Party Day!
- ☐ Have flowers delivered and arranged in the early morning.
- ☐ Finish decorations.
- ☐ Continue working with caterer.

You Are Cordially
Invited to
a Reception–Dinner
to Celebrate

The Marriage
of Our Daughter

November 15   *7 P.M.*

RSVP

*T*he quiet beauty of an at-home wedding reception–dinner gives family and guests a
chance to share the splendor of the day in an
intimate, hospitable setting. For fall or winter
weddings the key is to make the decor as inviting as a glowing fireplace and as sumptuous
as a formal banquet.

MENU

25–30 People

Open Bar

Beaujolais

Champagne

Water Chestnut Rumaki

* Cold Salmon Mousse

* Skewers of Chicken Saté with Peanut Sauce

* Fillet of Beef with Bearnaise Sauce

Rice Mold with Fresh Tomato Bits (Garnish with Fresh Baby Peas & Mushrooms)

Bibb & Endive Salad with Mustard Vinaigrette

Topiary Tree of Fresh Fruit

Coffee

Wedding Cake

Pastel Mints   *Sugared Pecans*

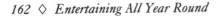

Invitations

Wedding invitations should be an expression of your spirit and your attitude toward this special occasion. You may want very formal engraved ones or something more off-beat. I feel that, whatever you choose, warm tones such as creamy ivory paper, and gold or brown lettering are very attractive for a fall or winter wedding.

SETTING THE STAGE

The most important part of planning this party is to make sure that traffic flow around the buffet and the seating areas is uncongested and comfortable. You need to have four distinct areas: the buffet, the bar, the dining tables, and an open area for conversation.

Buffet Table Centerpiece

<u>Props</u>

table, 12 feet long by 2½ to 3 feet wide
cranberry moiré tablecloth
2 silver candelabra with pink tapers
white birch branch, 54 to 60 inches long
Styrofoam, 10 inches high by 12 inches long
wooden flat, 20 by 20 inches
roll of flat moss, 30 by 30 inches
small portable battery pack
string of tiny white Christmas lights
36 small, capped bud vials
4 rubrum lilies, 3 cymbidium orchids, 10 red, purple, and white anemones, 6 peach colored roses, 5 dendrobium orchids, 4 gardenias
2 garlands of ivy, 3 feet long
floral wire
transparent plastic string

Setup

Cover table with moiré cloth.

Stick birch branch into center of Styrofoam. Secure.

Place battery pack next to Styrofoam. Connect lights.

Set battery pack and Styrofoam into wooden flat.

Cover flat and contents with moss.

String lights around birch branch.

Set aside 5 anemones, gardenias, and dendrobium orchids.

Insert the remaining flowers into bud vials. Cap. Flower stems should be cut very short.

Using leftover moss, cut it into strips 6 inches by 2 inches. Moisten. Wrap around each vial. Secure with green floral wire.

Take remaining flowers, do not cut stems,
and insert in remaining bud vials and wire
branches.
"Plant" vials across moss lawn at base of birch
by sinking vials into moss so they are
completely covered.
Set one candelabrum at each end of the
buffet.
Wrap ivy garlands around the stem and arms
of the candelabra; secure with floral wire.

The Buffet Food Presentation

Props

cut crystal platter
12-round glass plate
silver serving platter
silver gravy boat
silver carving platter
round silver serving plate
4 limes
2 dozen dried red chili peppers, 3 to 4 inches
long
head bib lettuce

Setup

Place salmon mousse on cut crystal platter.
Arrange Rumaki on a leaf lined round silver
serving plate.
Unmold rice on to large round glass plate.
Surround with garnish of fresh peas and
mushrooms.
Arrange chicken *saté* on silver platter
garnished with lime rounds and whole dried
red chili peppers on a bed of bib lettuce.
Set beef on carving platter. If serving cold,
pre-slice several portions. If serving hot,
have waiter in attendance to carve and
serve as needed. Place silver gravy boat
with bearnaise sauce to side of carving
platter.
Place dishes on separate small table covered
with a cranberry cloth. (Napkins and
silverware will be on dining tables.)

Individual Tables

<u>Props</u>

4 to 5 48-inch-round dining tables
floor length, round, cranberry moiré
   tablecloth per table
birch branch arrangement per table
10 peach colored roses, 10 cymbidium
   orchids, 10 rubrum lilies, 10 purple
   anemones, 10 pale freesias
deep cobalt-blue and gold place plates
cut glass wine goblets
cranberry linen napkins
two menu cards per table

<u>Setup</u>

Cover each table with the moiré cloth.
Set-up place plates, napkins, silverware, and
   goblets.

Write out two menu cards per table. Place them on small easels. They should identify the individual courses and clue guests into the organization of the meal.

Create birch branch arrangements. Follow instructions given under buffet table centerpiece. As a variation, try using only one type of flower (on the birch branch) per table. You create the rose table, the orchid table, etc. This allows you to set out seating cards on a separate table that guests can use to locate their places.

Special Touches

The wedding cake should be served from a separate table. It can be cut after the meal is cleared. Pass portions to seated guests.

COUNTDOWN

Two Months Before
- ☐ Draw up guest list.
- ☐ Mail invitations.
- ☐ Contact all caterers and party supply rental people.

One Month Before
- ☐ Set menu and sample all catered food. Adjust as needed.
- ☐ Order all flowers and props. Arrange for delivery the day of the party.

Two Weeks Before
- ☐ Have menu cards and place cards made up.
- ☐ Double check to make sure everything is going according to schedule.

One Week Before
- ☐ Double check that you have all cooking, serving, and dining supplies.

Two Days Before
- ☐ Have tables, chairs, dishes, and serving pieces delivered to house.

One Day Before
- ☐ Set-up basic buffet table, dining tables, and bar.
- ☐ Begin basic arrangements: set-up birch branches in flats and string lights.
- ☐ Prepare salmon mousse.
- ☐ Have flowers and moss delivered.
- ☐ Add to arrangements.

RECIPES

APPETIZERS

Beef Scallion Rolls

Makes 20 rolls

1 London broil, 2 inches thick (2½ pounds)
20 fresh scallions

Marinade
¾ cup sweet sherry
3 tablespoons orange juice concentrate
¼ cup vegetable oil
½ cup lemon juice
2 tablespoons Hoisin sauce
2 teaspoons soy sauce
1 teaspoon sesame oil
1 teaspoon Dijon mustard
½ medium Bermuda onion
1 clove garlic

◇ Combine marinade ingredients in blender or food processor until smooth.
◇ Marinate steak in sauce overnight, turning over from time to time.
◇ Broil steak 4 to 5 minutes per side. It should be rare.
◇ Slice steak into ⅛-inch-thick strips. Cut against the grain.
◇ Wash scallions. Trim ends so each stalk is 3 inches long.
◇ Feather green end of scallions. Make several 1-inch-long slashes along the length of the scallion tail.
◇ Wrap one slice of beef around each scallion. Secure with a toothpick.
◇ Serve at room temperature.

Cheese Straws

makes 4 dozen

10-ounce roll extrasharp process cheese, room temperature
½ cup (1 stick) butter, room temperature
1 cup flour
¼ to ½ teaspoon cayenne pepper, to taste
coarse salt, to taste
Worcestershire sauce, to taste (optional)

◇ Combine cheese and butter and mix well.
◇ Add remaining ingredients and blend. Chill until firm.
◇ Place on sheet of waxed paper and roll into a log about the diameter of a quarter. Freeze.
◇ Preheat oven to 350°F.
◇ Remove log from freezer and let sit at room temperature for 5 minutes.
◇ Cut log into strips ¼ inch thick and 3 to 6 inches long.
◇ Bake on a greased baking sheet for 10 minutes.
◇ Cool on wire racks.
◇ Store in airtight container.
(To refresh cheese straws, reheat in a 400°F oven for 2 to 3 minutes.)

Chicken Liver Paté

makes 1½ cups

1 pound fresh chicken livers
1 clove garlic, crushed
1 bay leaf, crushed
½ cup (1 stick) butter, room temperature
1 tablespoon corn oil
2 large shallots, finely minced
¼ cup onions, finely minced
½ cup fresh parsley, finely minced (optional)
sea salt and freshly ground pepper, to taste
1 to 2 tablespoons Cognac
3 tablespoons butter

◇ Toss chicken livers with garlic and bay leaf and place in the refrigerator overnight, or leave at room temperature for 1 to 2 hours.
◇ Heat 4 tablespoons butter with corn oil and sauté shallots and onions until soft but not browned.
◇ Wipe garlic and bay leaf mixture from chicken livers. Add livers to onions and shallots and cook over low heat until lightly browned but still a little pink in the center. Cool.
◇ In a blender or food processor, puree liver mixture.
◇ Add remaining 4 tablespoons butter, parsley, salt, pepper, and Cognac.
◇ Check seasoning.
◇ Spoon into buttered mold or ramekins and smooth top.
◇ Melt 3 tablespoons of butter and pour over pâté.
◇ Cover and refrigerate.
(This can be prepared 3 to 4 days in advance.)

Chicken *Saté* with Peanut Sauce

makes 10 8-inch skewers

2 whole chicken breasts (about 2 pounds each), boned, skinned, and cut into ¾-inch pieces

Marinade
⅓ cup soy sauce
3 tablespoons sesame oil
3 to 4 ⅛-inch-thick slices fresh ginger, minced
2 cloves garlic, crushed
2 tablespoons fresh lime juice

Peanut Sauce
1 cup peanuts, roasted
1 tablespoon sesame oil
1 small onion, finely chopped
2 cloves garlic, finely minced
1–2 small red chili peppers (to taste), finely minced
2 tablespoons fresh lime juice, or to taste
1 tablespoon soy sauce
1 ¼-inch slice fresh ginger, finely minced
boiling water

◇ Combine all marinade ingredients.
◇ Toss chicken pieces in marinade until coated.
◇ Let sit at room temperature for 1 hour; cover and refrigerate overnight.
◇ Remove chicken from marinade (reserve marinade) and thread 4 or 5 pieces onto each skewer.
◇ Heat sesame oil. Sauté onion and garlic until tender and golden.
◇ Transfer onions and garlic to a food processor or blender and add all remaining ingredients except water.
◇ Continue blending while slowly adding enough boiling water to make a paste that is dipping consistency.
◇ Pour peanut sauce into small saucepan and keep warm on low heat.
◇ Preheat broiler; place rack 4 inches from heat.
◇ Brush chicken with reserved marinade.
◇ Broil chicken until golden; about 4 to 5 minutes on each side.
◇ Serve with warm peanut sauce.

Cold Salmon Mousse

makes 3 cups

1/4 cup cold water
2 envelopes unflavored gelatin
1/2 cup juice drained from canned salmon
16-ounce can red salmon, drained (reserve juice), skin removed
Tabasco sauce, to taste
1/2 cup celery, finely chopped
2 tablespoons scallions, thinly sliced
2 to 3 tablespoons fresh lemon juice, to taste
2 to 3 tablespoons dried dill, to taste
sea salt, freshly ground white pepper, to taste
cayenne pepper, to taste
1 cup plain yogurt or whipped heavy cream
dried or fresh dill or thinly sliced cucumbers

◇ Place cold water and gelatin in small saucepan and let sit until gelatin is soft and spongy.
◇ Add salmon juice and stir over low heat until gelatin is completely dissolved.
◇ Cool completely.
◇ In a blender or food processor mix salmon and cooled gelatin for 1 to 2 minutes.
◇ Place mixture in refrigerator or in a bowl over ice water. Chill until it begins to set. Stir occasionally; you will feel it becoming stiffer.
◇ Add remaining ingredients, except yogurt, and stir.
◇ Fold in yogurt or whipped cream.
◇ Check seasoning.
◇ Pour into mold.
◇ Cover and refrigerate for 2 to 4 hours or until set.
◇ Unmold by running a knife around edges and inverting onto serving platter.
◇ Garnish with dill or cucumbers.
◇ Serve chilled.
    (This may be prepared a day in advance, covered, and refrigerated.)

Cold Shrimp with Soy Mustard Sauce

serves 15

3 pounds medium shrimp, peeled, washed, and deveined

Marinade
1 1/2 cups soy sauce
1/2 cup sesame oil
1/2 cup Dijon mustard
1 tablespoon grated or minced ginger
4 scallions, finely chopped

◇ Boil water in large pot. Cook shrimp for 3 to 4 minutes, until pink and firm. Do not overcook.
◇ Drain and cool.
◇ In a separate bowl, mix marinade ingredients with a whisk. Pour over shrimp, making sure they are coated. Refrigerate 4 to 6 hours, turning shrimp in marinade every hour or so.
◇ An hour before serving, remove from refrigerator. Serve shrimp skewered on toothpicks—2 or 3 per toothpick.

Curry Dip

makes 1 pint

1 tablespoon onion, finely chopped
1 tablespoon fresh parsley, finely minced
1 cup mayonnaise
1/2 cup sour cream
1 teaspoon Herb Seasoning
1 1/2 teaspoons fresh lemon juice
1/2 teaspoon Worcestershire sauce, or to taste
1/4 to 1/2 teaspoon curry powder, to taste
sea salt and pepper, to taste
2 teaspoons capers (optional)

◇ In a blender or food processor, combine all
   ingredients.
◇ Check seasoning.
◇ Let sit at room temperature about 1 hour to
   allow flavors to blend.
◇ Adjust seasoning.
◇ Cover and chill.
   (This can be prepared a couple of days
   in advance.)

Hot Cheese-Olive Puffs

makes 4 dozen

½ cup (1 stick) butter, room temperature
2 cups sharp cheddar cheese, grated, room
   temperature
1 cup flour
½ teaspoon salt
1 teaspoon paprika
7-ounce jar green stuffed olives, drained

◇ Preheat oven to 400°F.
◇ Mix cheese and butter until blended.
◇ Mix in flour, salt, and paprika.
◇ Shape (about) 1 tablespoon of cheese mixture around each olive, coating it completely.
◇ Place olives on baking sheet and bake 10 to
   12 minutes.
◇ Serve hot.
   (To prepare in advance, place unbaked
   cheese olives on a baking sheet, cover
   with plastic wrap or large plastic bags,
   and freeze. When ready to serve, place
   unwrapped sheets in hot oven for about
   20 minutes or until golden brown.)

Miniature Cheese Balls

makes 12

1 pound New York sharp cheddar cheese, grated,
   room temperature
4 ounces Roquefort cheese, room temperature
8 ounces cream cheese, room temperature
1 tablespoon Worcestershire sauce
1 tablespoon onion, grated
cayenne pepper, to taste
sea salt and freshly ground black pepper, to taste
¾ cup pecans, finely chopped

◇ Combine all ingredients except nuts and
   mix until smooth.
◇ Adjust seasoning. Chill.
◇ Shape into 12 balls.
◇ Place chopped nuts on waxed paper and
   roll cheese balls in nuts until completely
   coated.
◇ Serve at room temperature.

Ercole's Olive Appetizer

2 14-ounce jars green olives
2 10-ounce cans pitted black olives
1 small jar pimentos
2 stalks celery
1 green pepper
¼ cup olive oil
½ cup red wine vinegar
1 pinch oregano
1 clove garlic, crushed
salt and pepper to taste

◇ Mince olives, pimentos, celery, and green
   pepper by hand.
◇ Mix oil, vinegar, oregano, garlic, salt, and
   pepper.
◇ Combine olive and oil mixture; marinate
   overnight in airtight dish.
◇ Serve at room temperature.

Taramásalata

makes about 2 cups

8 to 10 slices bread, crusts removed
1 to 2 cloves garlic, finely minced, to taste
¼ cup taramá (carp or mullet roe, available at
  specialty food shops)
2 to 3 cups olive oil, to taste
juice of 2 to 3 lemons, to taste
2 egg yolks, beaten
cayenne pepper, to taste
fresh parsley, minced

◇ Soak bread in water and set aside.
◇ Combine garlic and *taramá* in a food pro-
  cessor or blender.
◇ Squeeze bread completely dry (discarding
  water) and add to *taramá* mixture; com-
  bine thoroughly.
◇ Add oil and lemon juice drop by drop, as
  for mayonnaise, while blending or pro-
  cessing until it takes on the consistency
  of a medium thick sauce.
◇ Add egg yolks and cayenne pepper; blend.
◇ Adjust seasoning.
◇ Cover with a thin film of olive oil; garnish
  with minced parsley. Chill.
◇ Serve with pita bread.
  (This can be prepared a day in advance.)

MAIN COURSES

Baked Eggs with Canadian Bacon

makes 1 serving

slice Canadian bacon, ¼ inch thick
2 eggs
1 tablespoon butter
1 teaspoon heavy cream
sea salt and freshly ground pepper, to taste

◇ Preheat oven to 350°F.
◇ Butter individual ramekin or custard cup.
◇ Trim bacon to fit ramekin or custard cup.
◇ Place bacon on bottom of ramekin and break eggs over top.
◇ Add butter, cream, salt, and pepper.
◇ Bake uncovered until eggs are firm but not hard, about 18 to 20 minutes.
◇ Serve in ramekin.
Variations:
Grated cheese, diced cooked vegetables, crumbled bacon, or diced ham can be substituted for the Canadian bacon.

Barbecued Shrimp in the Shells

serves 4 as main course or 10 to 12 as appetizer

½ cup (1 stick) butter, melted
¼ cup olive oil
2 cloves garlic, minced
2 bay leaves, crushed
1 teaspoon red pepper
1½ teaspoons paprika
½ teaspoon oregano
1 teaspoon basil
2 teaspoons fresh parsley, minced
¼ cup chili sauce
2 pounds large shrimp, unpeeled and uncooked, slit down the back

◇ Heat butter and oil in saucepan.
◇ Add remaining ingredients except shrimp, and cook over medium-low heat for 10 minutes. Cool.
◇ Place shrimp in shallow glass casserole.
◇ Pour marinade over shrimp and let sit 2 to 3 hours at room temperature, or refrigerate overnight. Toss occasionally.
◇ Preheat oven to 300°F.
◇ Bake shrimp in marinade just until they turn pink, about 15 minutes. Do not overbake!
◇ Serve hot. Have plenty of French bread on hand to soak up the sauce.

Chicken and Sausage Gumbo

serves 6

3 tablespoons peanut oil
3-pound chicken cut into 8 pieces, plus 1 whole
  chicken breast, halved
7 tablespoons bacon drippings
4 cups okra, cut into 1/2-inch slices
4 rounded tablespoons flour
2 cloves garlic, finely minced
1 medium onion, finely minced
3 stalks celery, chopped
1 green pepper, chopped
3 cups chicken stock
3 tablespoons tomato paste
1 pound can tomatoes, crushed (juice included)
1 teaspoon each thyme and basil
3 bay leaves
Tabasco sauce, to taste
sea salt and freshly ground pepper, to taste
2 smoked pork sausages, 5 inches long, 1 inch in
  diameter
4 to 5 green onions, thinly sliced
1/2 cup parsley, finely minced

◇ Heat peanut oil in large skillet and lightly
  brown chicken pieces on both sides; remove and drain on paper towels.
◇ Heat 3 tablespoons bacon drippings in a
  large pot and quickly sear okra slices,
  about 3 to 5 minutes over medium heat.
  Remove and set aside.
◇ Add remaining bacon drippings to pot,
  heat, and add flour. Stir constantly over
  medium heat until color of toasted walnut.
◇ Add garlic, onion, celery, and pepper and
  cook until vegetables are soft, about 10
  minutes.
◇ Add stock, tomato paste, tomatoes, spices,
  and seasonings and simmer covered for
  about 30 minutes. Uncover and cook another 10 minutes.
◇ Cut sausage into half-inch slices.
◇ Add chicken pieces, sausage, and okra.
  (Gumbo may be prepared to this point in
  advance, covered, and refrigerated. Be-

fore proceeding with next step, skim off
fat and allow gumbo to reach room temperature.)
◇ Cook covered 1 to 1½ hours; remove lid
  the last ½ hour.
◇ Check seasoning.
◇ Just before serving, add parsley and green
  onions.
◇ Serve in soup bowls over hot buttered rice.

Chili con Queso

serves 12 (about 2 cups)

2 tablespoons vegetable oil
1 medium onion, coarsely chopped
2 cloves garlic, finely minced
1/2 cup green bell pepper, diced
1 tablespoon flour
1/4 to 1/2 cup heavy cream, as needed
1 tablespoon flour
1/4 to 1/2 cup heavy cream, as needed
1 pound Monterey Jack or combination of
  Monterey Jack and Colby cheese, grated
sea salt and freshly ground pepper, to taste
1 tablespoon chili powder, or to taste
2 to 3 fresh jalapeño peppers, seeded and chopped,
  to taste

◇ In oil, sauté onion and garlic over medium
  heat until tender, about 5 minutes.
◇ Add green pepper and cook just until ten-
  der.
◇ Stir in flour and continue cooking about 1
  minute, stirring constantly.
◇ Reduce heat to low and add heavy cream,
  cheese, salt, pepper, and chili powder.
◇ Stir occasionally until cheeses are com-
  pletely melted.
◇ Stir in jalapeño peppers.
◇ Check seasoning.

Christmas Duckling

serves 2

4 to 5 pound duckling (excess fat, wings, and skin of neck removed)
sea salt and freshly ground pepper, as needed
1 stalk celery, coarsely chopped
½ onion, coarsely chopped
1 small carrot, coarsely chopped

◇ Preheat oven to 400°F.
◇ Season inside and outside of duck with salt and pepper. Stuff cavity with celery, onion, and carrot.
◇ Place duckling in roasting pan, breast side up. Roast for 1½ to 2 hours or until skin is crisp and brown and the juices run clear. Pour off accumulated fat during roasting period.
◇ Remove duckling from oven and let rest 15 minutes before carving.
◇ Split duck in half.
◇ Remove backbone and discard vegetables from cavity.

Cold Marinated Sea Scallops *en Brochette*

serves 6

2 limes
¼ cup olive oil
cayenne pepper, to taste
¾ pound fresh sea scallops
2 stalks celery
1 cucumber
12 cherry tomatoes
6 6-inch wooden skewers

◇ Combine lime juice, olive oil, and cayenne pepper.
◇ Wash scallops and cut in half lengthwise.
◇ Cover scallops with lime–oil marinade and refrigerate in airtight bowl for 2 hours.
◇ Cut celery into ½-inch wide chunks.

◇ Peel cucumber. Cut lengthwise and remove seeds. Cut into cubes.
◇ Add celery, cucumber, and tomatoes to scallops in marinade. Toss.
◇ Allow to sit for 10 minutes.
◇ Alternate vegetables and scallops on the skewers. Chill before serving.

Crab Mornay

serves 2 to 4

1 cup béchamel sauce (see page 176)
2 tablespoons butter
2 shallots, finely minced
¼ cup celery, finely minced
¼ cup green bell pepper, finely minced
1 pound fresh crab meat, drained
3 tablespoons sherry
Worcestershire sauce, to taste
sea salt and freshly ground white pepper, to taste
dash of cayenne pepper
¼ to ½ cup fresh bread crumbs, as needed
½ cup imported Swiss cheese, grated

◇ Prepare béchamel sauce and set aside.
◇ Melt butter and sauté shallots, celery, and green pepper over low heat until soft but not browned.
◇ Combine béchamel, celery–pepper mixture, crab meat, sherry, Worcestershire sauce, salt, and peppers.
◇ Check seasoning.
◇ Spoon into buttered scallop shell or individual baking dishes.
◇ Sprinkle each with bread crumbs, then top with grated cheese. (This can be prepared hours ahead, covered, and refrigerated.)
◇ Preheat oven to 375°F.
◇ Bake 10 to 15 minutes or until bubbling and golden brown.

Crown Roast of Pork

serves 6

6 to 7 pound crown roast of pork, at room
  temperature
¼ cup melted butter
¼ cup corn oil
2 cloves garlic, slivered
freshly ground pepper, to taste
sea salt, to taste

◊ Preheat oven to 400°F.
◊ Pat roast dry with paper towels. Combine melted butter and corn oil and brush on roast.
◊ With a sharp knife, make several slits in roast and insert garlic slivers at random.
◊ Season well with fresh pepper.
◊ Wrap rib tips with pieces of foil to keep them from charring. Place roast in shallow roasting pan, bone ends up.
◊ Roast for 10 minutes, then reduce heat to 325°F. Bake 25 minutes per pound or until internal temperature reaches 165°F to 170°F. (To test internal roast temperature, insert meat thermometer deep into the thickest part of the roast, without touching bone, about 30 minutes prior to serving. Roast will continue to cook after it is removed from oven.)
◊ Season roast with salt about 30 minutes before done.
◊ Transfer roast to warmed serving platter.
◊ Remove foil from rib tips; let rest 15 minutes before carving.

Eggs Florentine

serves 8

butter
2 cups Mornay sauce
3 to 4 packages frozen spinach in butter or frozen
  spinach in cream, cooked and drained well
sea salt and freshly ground pepper, to taste
8 to 16 eggs, poached
½ cup Gruyère or Swiss cheese, grated

◊ Butter 8 ramekins or a 6 to 8-inch au gratin dish.
◊ Place a spoonful of sauce on bottom of dish.
◊ Season spinach with salt and pepper and divide evenly among ramekins.
◊ Preheat broiling unit.
◊ Drain poached eggs. Place over layer of spinach.
◊ Spoon Mornay sauce over eggs and sprinkle grated cheese over top.
◊ Place ramekins on a baking sheet and heat under the broiler until sauce is bubbly and cheese is melted.

Mornay Sauce *(2 cups)*
3 tablespoons butter
3 tablespoons flour
1½ cups milk
cayenne pepper, to taste
sea salt and freshly ground white pepper, to taste
freshly ground nutmeg, to taste
½ cup heavy cream
½ cup Gruyère or Swiss cheese, freshly grated

◊ Melt butter in saucepan. Add flour and cook over medium heat for 1 to 2 minutes, stirring constantly.
◊ Add milk and continue whisking briskly over medium heat until sauce thickens.
◊ Add seasonings, cream, and grated cheese; stir.
◊ Adjust seasoning.
  (If a thinner sauce is desired, stir in an additional ¼ cup cream or milk.)

Variations:
Béchamel Sauce: Omit the cheese.
Aurore Sauce: Omit the cheese; add ⅓ cup fresh seeded and diced tomatoes or tomato puree.
Velouté Sauce: Omit the cheese; substitute beef, chicken, or fish stock for half or all of the milk.

Fillet of Beef

serves 10

1 beef tenderloin (about 4½ pounds), barded and
    tied, room temperature
freshly ground pepper, to taste
fresh garlic, minced, to taste (optional)
sea salt, to taste

◇ Preheat oven to 400°F.
◇ Season tenderloin with pepper and garlic.
◇ Place on broiling rack and roast 45 minutes
    for rare.
◇ After roasting for 30 minutes, season with
    salt.
◇ Remove from oven and let rest at least 15
    minutes before carving.
◇ Remove strings and barding fat.
◇ Carve into thin slices.

Honey-Batter Fried Chicken

makes 10 pieces

3 cloves garlic, finely minced
1 medium onion, finely minced
2 tablespoons butter
juice of 2 lemons
½ cup honey
⅓ cup Dijon mustard
1 teaspoon ginger, to taste
cayenne pepper, to taste
freshly ground pepper, to taste
10 pieces chicken—10 breast halves, 10 legs, or a
    combination of the two
salt and pepper
flour
peanut oil to make depth of 1 inch in fry pan

◇ Sauté garlic and onions in hot butter over
    low heat until soft but not browned.
    Pour into a glass casserole, approx-
    imately 8 by 13 inches.
◇ Add lemon juice, honey, mustard, ginger,
    and cayenne and fresh ground peppers.
    Mix.
◇ Add chicken pieces to marinade, coating
    thoroughly.
◇ Refrigerate overnight. Turn occasionally.
◇ Remove chicken from refrigerator and al-
    low to reach room temperature.
◇ Salt and pepper each chicken piece and let
    drain for 5 to 10 minutes on a wire rack.
◇ Coat completely with flour; shake away ex-
    cess.
◇ Heat oil to sizzling over medium heat and
    brown chicken on both sides, about 5
    minutes on each side. Don't crowd in fry
    pan.
◇ Remove pieces and drain.
◇ Place in a baking pan and continue baking
    at 350°F for 20 minutes. (The honey
    coating will cause chicken to brown
    more, so watch carefully.)

Individual Chicken Curry Rice Casseroles

makes 12 5-inch casseroles

2 packages (6 ounces each) long grain and wild
  rice mix
3 tablespoons butter
3 cups velouté sauce (see page 176)
3 cups chopped broccoli, blanched and drained
6 cups cooked chicken, cut into bite sized pieces
1½ cups mayonnaise
¾ cup light cream
1½ to 2 teaspoons curry powder, to taste
sea salt and freshly ground white pepper, to taste
1 cup water chestnuts, sliced
1½ cups imported Swiss cheese, grated

◇ Prepare rice as package directs; add butter
  and set aside.
◇ Prepare velouté sauce and set aside.
◇ Preheat oven to 350°F.
◇ Divide rice evenly among 12 buttered indi-
  vidual casseroles or soup bowls.
◇ Place a layer of broccoli over rice.
◇ Layer chicken pieces over broccoli.
◇ Combine velouté sauce, mayonnaise, cream,
  and seasonings; blend.
◇ Adjust seasoning.
◇ Spoon a layer of velouté mixture over
  chicken.
◇ Sprinkle water chestnuts over sauce.
◇ Top with grated cheese.
◇ Bake 20 minutes or until hot and bubbly.
  (This can be prepared 1 to 2 days in ad-
  vance, covered, and refrigerated. It can
  also be frozen, brought to room tempera-
  ture, then baked.)

Leg of Lamb Mediterranean

serves 8 to 10

5- to 7-pound leg of lamb with shank attached
fresh parsley

Marinade
2 cloves garlic, minced
1 medium onion, chopped
1 piece of ginger, size of a quarter, peeled and
  finely minced
2 teaspoons ground coriander
1 teaspoon fresh thyme
1 teaspoon fresh savory
1 teaspoon ground cumin
½ cup fresh coriander, chopped
1 tablespoon black pepper, freshly ground
2 tablespoons sea salt
¼ to ½ cup olive oil
½ cup fresh lemon juice

◇ Dry leg of lamb with paper towels and
  place in shallow glass baking dish.
◇ Combine marinade ingredients in a bowl.
  Pour over lamb. Spread marinade until
  roast is evenly covered.
◇ Let sit at room temperature for 1 hour; turn
  roast and let sit another hour.
◇ Cover with plastic wrap and refrigerate
  overnight, turning occasionally. (Lamb
  can marinate up to 2 days.)
◇ Remove from refrigerator, drain, and allow
  to reach room temperature.
◇ Preheat oven to 450°F.
◇ Roast fat side up for 10 minutes; reduce
  heat to 350°F and continue roasting until
  internal temperature is 150° for medium
  (about 1½ hours at 12 to 15 minutes per
  pound. Allow about 10 minutes per
  pound for rare; about 20 minutes per
  pound for well done.)
◇ Let rest on serving platter at least 15 minutes before carving.
◇ Garnish with fresh parsley.

Marinated London Broil

serves 4

1 to 2 pound flank steak, room temperature
1 tablespoon vegetable oil
½ cup soy sauce
¼ cup red wine or sherry
¼ cup fresh orange juice
1 teaspoon fresh ginger, finely minced
2 cloves garlic, finely minced
grated rind of 1 orange
dash of freshly ground pepper
3 tablespoons cold water
1 teaspoon corn starch

◇ Place steak in a glass baking dish.
◇ Combine oil, soy sauce, wine, orange juice, ginger, garlic, and orange rind; pour over steak.
◇ Cover and refrigerate overnight or marinate 3 to 4 hours at room temperature.
◇ Preheat broiling unit. Place oven rack about 3 inches from heat.
◇ Drain steak, reserving marinade, and place on broiling tray.
◇ In a small pan, cook strained marinade over medium heat until it comes to a boil.
◇ Combine water and cornstarch and add to marinade; stir until thick. Keep warm.
◇ Broil steak 3½ minutes on each side for medium rare. (Flank steak should always be cooked rare, as it toughens and becomes dry with continued cooking.)
◇ Season lightly with pepper.
◇ Let rest 3 to 5 minutes before carving.
◇ Slice thinly, across the grain (on the diagonal).
◇ Serve immediately with warm sauce.

Pasta Primavera

serves 6 to 8

4 cups fresh zucchini, cut into 1½-inch strips
   (approximately 3 medium sized zucchinis)
2 cups fresh broccoli in bite sized pieces
1 cup fresh peas or 10 ounces frozen peas, thawed,
   not cooked
1 red bell pepper, cut into 1½-inch strips
4 cups fresh green beans, cut into 1½-inch lengths
4 to 6 tablespoons olive oil, to taste
2 to 3 cloves garlic, finely minced, to taste
2 medium tomatoes, peeled, seeded, and diced
¼ cup fresh basil, finely minced
3 to 4 tablespoons red wine vinegar, to taste
sea salt and freshly ground pepper, to taste
1 pound linguine
black olives, pitted and chopped (optional)

◇ Blanch each vegetable separately in boiling, salted water for 1 to 2 minutes or until just crisp-tender. Refresh in cold water; drain and set aside.
◇ Heat 2 to 3 tablespoons olive oil in large skillet (big enough to hold all the vegetables) and cook garlic over low heat until soft but not browned.
◇ Add tomatoes and sauté over medium heat for 2 to 3 minutes.
◇ Remove from heat and pour into large serving bowl (big enough to hold pasta and vegetables).
◇ Cook pasta in large pot of boiling water (about 6 to 7 quarts) until *al dente*, about 8 to 12 minutes; drain and set aside.
◇ Heat remaining olive oil in skillet and quickly reheat all the drained vegetables.
◇ Add drained pasta and heated vegetables to tomato mixture; toss until pasta is lightly coated.
◇ Add basil, wine vinegar, salt, and pepper to pasta.
◇ Adjust seasoning.
◇ Garnish with chopped olives if desired.
◇ Serve at room temperature.

Pita Pockets with Chicken and Mozzarella Cheese

serves 8

4 to 8 pita rounds (depending on size)
1/2 cup garlic-seasoned olive oil
1 to 1 1/2 pounds mozzarella cheese, thinly sliced
1 1/2 pounds baked chicken breasts, thinly sliced or shredded
4 medium tomatoes, peeled, seeded, and diced
fresh basil, finely minced
scallions (green part included), thinly sliced
fresh basil leaves
cherry tomatoes

◇ Cut or tear pita rounds in half (or cut the tops off if they are small); brush interiors with garlic-seasoned olive oil.
◇ Arrange cheese, chicken, diced tomatoes, basil, and scallions on a platter.
◇ Garnish platter with fresh basil leaves and cherry tomatoes.

Pizza

makes 15-inch pizza

1 package dry yeast
1 teaspoon sugar
1/2 cup warm water (110°F)
1 1/4 cups unsifted, unbleached flour
1 teaspoon salt
1 tablespoon vegetable oil

◇ Grease a 15-inch pizza pan or baking sheet.
◇ Dissolve yeast and sugar in warm water in a cup and set aside for 5 to 10 minutes or until mixture becomes frothy and swollen.
◇ Place flour and salt in a food processor and process 2 to 3 seconds using a metal blade.
◇ Turn the processor on and pour yeast mixture into the flour.

◇ Process the dough until it starts to pull away from the sides of the bowl, about 1 minute.
◇ Add oil and process for 1 minute more, or until dough leaves sides of bowl. (Dough will be soft and moist. If it sticks to sides of processor bowl, add flour, one tablespoon at a time, and process until it pulls away from sides.)
◇ Sprinkle dough with flour and store in plastic bag in the refrigerator for 1 hour. (Dough can be prepared up to 1 day in advance.)
◇ Preheat oven to 425°F.
◇ Roll dough into a 15-inch circle and place on pizza pan.
◇ Cover dough with plastic wrap and let rise 20 minutes.
◇ Add tomato sauce and desired toppings.
◇ Bake for 20 minutes or until bottom crust is golden.
◇ Cut into wedges and serve.
   (If pizza dough is prepared by hand, combine the ingredients in a bowl. Knead the dough on a lightly floured surface for 5 to 10 minutes or until smooth and elastic. Then store in refrigerator for 1 hour before proceeding with rest of recipe.

Tomato Sauce
2 tablespoons olive oil
1 medium clove garlic, finely minced
1 medium onion, chopped
30-ounce can whole Italian tomatoes, chopped (juice included)
3 tablespoons tomato paste
1 teaspoon oregano, crushed
dried chili pepper (optional)
sea salt and freshly ground pepper, to taste

◇ In oil sauté garlic and onions over medium heat until they become soft but not browned.
◇ Add remaining ingredients and cook covered over medium heat for 5 to 10 minutes, stirring occasionally.
◇ Reduce heat to low and cook for 45 to 60 minutes or until thick.
◇ Adjust seasoning.

Rolled Boneless Leg of Lamb with Mint Stuffing

serves 10*

1 leg of baby lamb (5–7 pounds), boned and trimmed
5 garlic cloves, cut into thin slivers
juice of two lemons
1 cup fresh mint leaves, finely chopped
salt and pepper to taste
1 cup red wine

◊ Lay lamb out flat. With sharp knife, make a dozen cuts in meat. Insert garlic slivers.
◊ Pour lemon juice evenly over meat. Sprinkle mint, salt, and pepper.
◊ Roll meat in a jelly roll fashion and tie securely with string.
◊ Preheat oven to 325°F.
◊ Place on rack in roasting pan. Roast (allow 20 minutes per pound), basting from time to time. After 1 hour, baste with wine. Continue basting until done.
◊ When lamb is cooked, open oven door and allow it to sit for 10 minutes. Remove string and bring lamb to the table. Cut in thin slices.

   *Recipe can be doubled or tripled if necessary.

Shrimp Aurore in Puff Pastry Shells

serves 5

1 cup velouté sauce (see page 176; use fish stock)
1 large shallot, finely minced
2 tablespoons butter
½ cup heavy cream
1 pound baby shrimp, drained
1 medium fresh tomato, peeled, seeded, and finely diced
1 cup fresh peas cooked, or frozen peas thawed, drained, and not cooked
sea salt and freshly ground white pepper, to taste
cayenne pepper, to taste
purchased puff pastry shells

◊ Prepare *velouté* sauce and set aside.
◊ Sauté shallots in butter over low heat until translucent.
◊ Add cream and cook 5 minutes over medium heat; stir occasionally.
◊ Add *velouté* sauce and mix.
◊ Add shrimp and cook just until opaque, 2 to 3 minutes. Don't overcook!
◊ Add tomato, peas, salt, and peppers; cook just until heated.
◊ Check seasoning.
◊ Serve hot over puff pastry shells.
   (This can be made several hours in advance, covered, and refrigerated.)

Variation:
Serve over a bed of hot rice instead of a pastry shell.

Spinach and Cheese Quiche

makes 1 9-inch deep dish quiche

1 recipe pastry dough (see page 203)
uncooked beans or rice
1 egg, beaten
2 tablespoons scallions, finely minced
2 tablespoons butter
10 ounces frozen chopped spinach, thawed and
* drained*
3 eggs, room temperature
1½ cups heavy cream
sea salt and freshly ground white pepper, to taste
nutmeg, to taste
⅓ cup imported Swiss cheese, grated
2 tablespoons unsalted butter, cut into pieces

◊ Preheat oven to 400°F.
◊ Grease a 9-inch removable bottom tart pan; line with dough. Cover with waxed paper; fill with dried beans or rice.
◊ Place tart pan on baking sheet and bake for 10 minutes, or until pastry begins to shrink from sides of pan.
◊ Remove waxed paper and beans.
◊ Prick bottom of pastry with fork.
◊ Brush pastry with beaten egg and return to oven for an additional 3 to 4 minutes.
◊ Remove tart pan from baking sheet and cool. (Partially baked pastry can be prepared several hours in advance.)
◊ Reduce oven heat to 375°F.
◊ Sauté scallions in hot butter until soft but not browned.
◊ Add spinach and stir over medium heat until water evaporates; cool.
◊ In a bowl, combine eggs, cream, and seasonings; mix until blended.
◊ Gradually stir spinach into egg mixture.
◊ Pour into pastry shell; sprinkle top with cheese and butter.
◊ Bake 25 to 30 minutes or until knife inserted in the center comes out clean.

Variation:
Ham and Mushroom Quiche: Substitute 10 ounces sautéed fresh mushrooms for the chopped spinach; add ⅓ cup diced ham.

Stuffed Breast of Veal

serves 6 to 8

3 tablespoons olive oil
3 tablespoons freshly ground pepper
2 cloves garlic, finely minced
3½ pound breast of veal, boned, room
* temperature*
1½ pounds lean pork, ground
1½ cups fresh parsley, finely chopped
2 cloves garlic, finely chopped
½ cup scallions, chopped
1½ to 2 cups bread crumbs, toasted
1 egg, lightly beaten
1 teaspoon thyme
sea salt and freshly ground pepper, to taste
freshly ground pepper and olive oil
1 carrot, 1 stalk celery, 1 small onion, and
* handful of parsley, coarsely chopped*

◊ Combine olive oil, pepper, and garlic and brush over veal; refrigerate covered overnight.
◊ Combine pork, parsley, garlic, scallions, bread crumbs, egg, salt, and pepper.
◊ Spoon stuffing down center of boned side of breast. (Stuffing will be about 3 inches wide.)
◊ Bring sides of meat to center (covering or overlapping stuffing); using a trussing needle and cotton string, sew or seam the sides together.
◊ Preheat oven to 450°F.
◊ Mix pepper and olive oil.
◊ Place roast in roasting pan; brush with olive oil mixture; cover with foil.
◊ Roast 30 minutes; remove foil. Slide chopped vegetable mixture under roast.
◊ Re-cover roast; lower heat to 350°F and continue roasting for 1½ hours.
  (To test for doneness, insert a sharp knife into thickest part of meat. If juices run clear, the roast is done.)
◊ Remove string and let rest 15 minutes before carving.

◇ Make a sauce by straining or pureeing the roasting juices and cooking over medium heat until desired consistency is reached.
◇ Adjust seasoning.
◇ Pour sauce over roast slices.

Sugar Glazed Baked Ham

serves 12 to 15

1½ cups brown sugar, packed
1 teaspoon cinnamon
½ to 1 teaspoon ginger, to taste
1 tablespoon flour
2 tablespoons brandy
cayenne pepper, to taste
Dijon mustard
5 to 7 pounds semiboneless smoked ham (preferably the shank half)
handful of cloves

◇ Preheat oven to 325°F.
◇ Combine sugar, cinnamon, ginger, flour, brandy, and pepper.
◇ Add enough mustard to make a thick paste that will adhere to the ham.
◇ Reserve 2 to 3 tablespoons of paste; spread remaining paste evenly over the entire ham.
◇ Place ham on broiling rack in a large, shallow roasting pan containing 1½ inches of hot water.
◇ Make an aluminum foil tent over ham and bake for 1½ to 2 hours.
◇ The last 10 to 15 minutes of baking, remove foil and score the fat in a diamond pattern, cutting in 1-inch intervals; stud ham with cloves inserted at points of the diamond.
◇ Spread remaining paste over top and bake at 500°F, or broil until glaze becomes golden brown.
◇ Remove ham from oven.
◇ Let rest at least 15 minutes before carving.

Texas Chili

serves 12

2 cups dried pinto or kidney beans
2 to 3 cloves garlic, finely minced
2 medium onions, coarsely chopped
2 tablespoons olive oil
4 pounds lean chuck or round steak, coarsely ground
1 teaspoon ground oregano
2 teaspoons cumin powder
3 to 4 tablespoons chili powder, to taste
2 to 3 20-ounce cans of tomatoes, crushed (juice included)
red hot sauce, to taste
2 cups hot water
sea salt and freshly ground pepper, to taste

◇ Soak beans overnight. Cook as package directs; reserve broth.
◇ Sauté garlic and onions in hot oil over medium heat until soft but not browned.
◇ Add meat and cook over high heat until it is lightly browned.
◇ Drain fat.
◇ Add oregano, cumin, chili powder, tomatoes, hot sauce, water, salt, and pepper and bring to a boil.
◇ Simmer covered for 30 minutes.
◇ Add beans (including broth) and simmer uncovered over medium heat for 1 hour or until desired consistency is reached.
◇ Adjust seasoning.
   (For best flavor, prepare chili 2 to 3 days in advance and store covered in refrigerator.)

Turkey with Cornbread-Sausage Stuffing

serves 16 to 18

*4 to 5 cups of your favorite cornbread, crumbled
and dried overnight*
*½–equal portion of toasted bread, crumbled and
dried overnight*
1 pound pork sausage, crumbled
*1 sweet pepper, chopped (canned pimentos can be
substituted)*
3 medium onions, chopped
6 to 8 celery stalks with leaves, chopped
1 to 3 tablespoons dried sage, crumbled, to taste
1 bunch fresh parsley, minced
sea salt and freshly ground pepper, to taste
about 1½ cups chicken stock
*20 to 25 pound turkey, giblets removed, room
temperature*
sea salt and freshly ground pepper
½ cup (1 stick) butter, melted

◇ Combine toast and cornbread in a large
bowl.
◇ Sauté sausage until partially cooked; add
pepper, onions, celery; cook until soft
but not browned.
◇ Drain accumulated fat and add sausage
mixture to bread mixture.
◇ Add sage, parsley, salt, and pepper.
◇ Add stock gradually until mixture feels
slightly moist. (It should be neither too
moist nor too dry.)

◇ Adjust seasoning.
◇ Preheat oven to 350°F.
◇ Dry turkey and cavity with paper towels.
◇ Season cavity with salt and pepper; fill with
stuffing mixture.
◇ Sew up cavity; brush turkey with melted
butter.
◇ Place turkey on rack in shallow roasting
pan; roast for ½ hour.
◇ Lower heat to 325°F and continue roasting
for 4 to 5 hours, or until thermometer
inserted into the thickest part of inside
thigh registers 180°F (about 13 to 15
minutes per pound).
◇ Baste turkey breast occasionally. (If turkey
becomes too brown, cover with an aluminum foil tent.)
◇ The turkey is done when the juices that
run out are clear, or when the drumstick
joint moves easily. (Don't overcook.)
◇ Place turkey on serving platter; remove
string and let rest 15 to 20 minutes before carving.

VEGETABLES AND SIDE DISHES

Artichoke Bisque

serves 6

3 tablespoons butter
¼ cup onions, minced
8½ ounce can artichoke hearts in water, drained
* and quartered*
2 large scallions, including some green tops
2 stalks celery, chopped
2 cups chicken stock
1 cup heavy cream
freshly ground nutmeg, to taste
sea salt and freshly ground white pepper, to taste
dash of cayenne pepper (optional)
chives or dill, minced

◇ Melt butter in heavy saucepan; add onions
    and cook over low heat until onions are
    translucent, 5 to 8 minutes.
◇ Add artichokes, scallions, and celery; cook
    uncovered for 5 minutes over medium
    heat.
◇ Cover; cook over low heat for about 15
    minutes.
◇ Add stock; cover and continue cooking for
    30 minutes or until vegetables are ten-
    der. Cool.
◇ Using a blender or food processor, puree
    soup in small batches.
◇ Return puree to saucepan; add heavy
    cream and seasonings.
◇ Stir over low heat until warmed through.
    Do not let boil.
◇ Garnish with chives or dill.
◇ Serve hot or chilled.

Artichoke Bottoms with Broccoli Puree

serves 2

15-ounce can artichoke bottoms, drained
1 bunch fresh broccoli, stems and flowerets
5 tablespoons butter, room temperature
1 to 2 tablespoons heavy cream
sea salt and freshly ground pepper, to taste
dash of nutmeg, freshly grated

◇ Sauté artichokes in butter until tender and
    set aside.
◇ Steam broccoli until tender.
◇ Process broccoli in a food processor or
    blender until coarsely chopped.
◇ Add 4 tablespoons butter, cream, salt, pep-
    per, and nutmeg; process or blend to de-
    sired consistency.
◇ Check seasoning.
◇ Place puree and remaining butter in sauce-
    pan and heat briefly.
◇ Mound puree on artichoke bottoms.
◇ Serve hot.

Baked Onions

serves 6

6 medium whole onions
3 slices bacon
½ to ¾ cups brown sugar, packed
6 tablespoons butter
6 toothpicks
sea salt and freshly ground white pepper, to taste

◇ Preheat oven to 350°F.
◇ Slice off both ends of onions; peel. Make a deep cross-shaped cut in top of each.
◇ Wrap ½ slice of bacon around the top of each onion. Secure with toothpicks.
◇ Divide sugar evenly over the scored tops of each onion.
◇ Place pat of butter on top of sugar; season with salt and pepper.
◇ Place in a casserole dish and bake covered for 1 hour.
◇ Before serving, remove toothpicks.

Brown Rice Exotica

serves 8

2 tablespoons butter or oil
1 onion, finely chopped
⅓ cup pine nuts
2 cups short grain brown rice
4½ cups chicken bouillon
½ cup raisins
salt to taste
1 teaspoon allspice

◇ Heat butter until it bubbles. Add onion, stirring until it is barely golden. Add pine nuts and sauté 1 minute longer, until both onion and pine nuts are lightly browned.
◇ Add rice, bouillon, raisins, salt, and allspice. Bring to a boil, cover, and cook over low flame for 30 to 45 minutes, depending on quality of rice.
◇ When rice is done, fluff up and serve.

Chili Beans

serves 10

1 tablespoon bacon drippings
1 medium onion, minced
1 pound chuck or sirloin steak, ground
2 32-ounce cans baked beans
2 tablespoons sugar
2 tablespoons vinegar
½ cup catsup (see Mary's Homemade Catsup, page 189)
2 teaspoons chili powder, to taste
sea salt and freshly ground pepper, to taste
cayenne pepper, to taste

◇ Preheat oven to 300°F.
◇ Heat bacon drippings and sauté onions over low heat until soft but not brown.
◇ Add ground meat and cook over medium high heat until browned.
◇ Drain off grease.
◇ Add remaining ingredients and stir.
◇ Check seasoning.
◇ Pour into 2 quart casserole and bake for 1 hour. (This may be prepared several days in advance.)

Creole Cabbage

serves 8 to 10

1 large head cabbage, cored and quartered
3 slices soft bread, crusts removed and toasted
½ cup milk
1 tablespoon corn oil
¼ cup (½ stick) butter
4 small garlic cloves, finely minced
2 medium onions, finely chopped
½ cup green onions, chopped
1 green pepper, chopped
4 celery stalks, chopped
½ pound cheddar cheese, grated
1 cup heavy cream
¼ cup parsley, minced

◇ Parboil cabbage in pot of boiling, salted water until barely tender, about 8 minutes. Drain well. Wrap in towel to dry completely.
◇ Soak toasted bread in milk and set aside.
◇ Melt oil and butter in a large saucepan over medium heat.
◇ Add garlic, onions, pepper, and celery; sauté until limp, not browned.
◇ Add cabbage and cook about 10 minutes, stirring occasionally.
◇ Squeeze milk out of bread mixture. Discard milk. Add bread, along with ½ of the cheese, to the cabbage.
◇ Cook cabbage mixture a few minutes; then remove from heat.
◇ Add cream and parsley and mix well.
◇ Pour into a greased 9- by 13-inch casserole and top with remaining cheese.
◇ Bake uncovered in a 350°F oven for 30 minutes. (This can be made the day before, covered, and refrigerated.)

Herb Buttered Italian Bread

serves 6 to 8

10 tablespoons butter, softened
½ teaspoon garlic powder, to taste
1 tablespoon each fresh parsley, chives, and basil, finely minced
fresh lemon juice, to taste
1 loaf Italian bread, unsliced

◇ Preheat oven to 400°F.
◇ Combine butter, garlic powder, parsley, chives, and basil.
◇ Add lemon juice and check seasoning.
◇ Slice bread vertically into 1-inch slices, without slicing through the bottom layer of crust.
◇ Spread herb butter on both sides of slices.
◇ Wrap bread in foil and bake for 10 minutes.

Mary's Homemade Catsup

makes 3 pints

12 cups ripe tomatoes (about 14 tomatoes), peeled and cored
6 medium onions, chopped coarsely
2 cloves garlic, minced
4 red bell peppers, chopped
2 hot red peppers, seeded and minced
2 cups brown sugar
4 bay leaves, crumbled
1 stick cinnamon, crushed
2 teaspoons each mustard seed, white peppercorns, whole allspice (crushed with a mortar and pestle)
1 teaspoon whole cloves
2 cups cider vinegar
2 teaspoons salt

◇ Cook tomatoes, onions, garlic, and peppers in a large noncorrosive, covered kettle over medium heat until softened; about 30 minutes. Stir occasionally and crush tomatoes with back of spoon.
◇ Process mixture through a sieve or food mill and return to kettle.
◇ Add sugar, bay leaves, cinnamon, mustard seed, peppercorns, allspice, and cloves; continue cooking, uncovered, stirring occasionally until reduced to half the original amount (45 minutes or more, depending on size of kettle and juiciness of tomatoes).
◇ Process mixture once again through a food mill, discarding spices; return to kettle.
◇ Add vinegar and salt.
◇ Cook over medium heat until mixture is reduced to the consistency of a thick puree; stir occasionally to prevent scorching.
◇ Pour into sterilized jars and process according to manufacturer's instructions. (Hot water bath requires 35 minutes.)
◇ Let catsup age a few weeks to allow flavors to blend.
(The consistency of homemade catsup is not as homogenized as store-bought; it is coarser and can be as spicy as you like.)

Ols Fashioned Coleslaw

serves 10 to 12

1 medium head cabbage, finely shredded, 7 to 9
  cups
1 tablespoon salt
1 medium onion, finely chopped
1 green pepper, diced
1 carrot, shredded
1/2 cup sugar
3/4 cup vinegar
2 to 2 1/2 teaspoons celery seed
sea salt and freshly ground pepper, to taste

◇ Combine shredded cabbage with salt and
  let drain for 1 hour. Squeeze out extra
  water.
◇ Combine cabbage, onion, pepper, and carrot in a large bowl and set aside.
◇ Combine sugar, vinegar, celery seed, salt,
  and pepper in a saucepan; boil for 1 minute. Cool.
◇ Pour over cabbage mixture and store covered in refrigerator.
  (This can be prepared several days in advance.)

Country Style Green Beans

serves 4

2 pounds string beans (half runners preferably)
6 cups water, or enough to cover beans by 1 inch
6 to 8 ounces salt pork, quartered (or a smoked
  ham hock)
1 medium onion, finely minced
1/2 teaspoon thyme
sea salt and freshly ground pepper, to taste

◇ Wash and string beans and break into 2-
  inch lengths.
◇ Bring water, salt pork, onion, thyme, salt
  and pepper to a boil; simmer for 10 to 15
  minutes.
◇ Add beans to water; cover. Cook over medium heat until water comes to a boil.
◇ Reduce heat; cook until tender. Time var-
  ies from 1 to 3 hours, depending on type
  and age of bean.
◇ Adjust seasoning.

Potatoes Anna

serves 6

2 tablespoons peanut oil
6 tablespoons butter, melted
8 medium potatoes, peeled and sliced 1/8 inch thick
sea salt and freshly ground pepper, to taste

◇ Grease well a heavy, round-bottomed skil-
  let with oven-proof handle.
◇ Preheat oven to 450°F.
◇ Heat oil and 2 tablespoons butter until hot.
◇ Arrange potato slices overlapping in circles
  on the bottom of the pan.
◇ Season with salt, pepper, and rest of but-
  ter.
◇ Repeat layers until all potatoes are used
  and the skillet is full.
◇ Cook uncovered over medium heat for 10
  to 15 minutes or until potatoes are
  browned on the bottom.
◇ Cover; place in oven for 10 minutes.
◇ Uncover potatoes; lower heat to 400°F.
  Cook 10 to 15 minutes or until bottom is
  browned and potatoes are tender.
◇ Remove hot skillet from oven; drain
  grease.
◇ Run metal spatula around edge of skillet to
  insure easy removal of potatoes.
◇ Invert potatoes on serving platter.

Sweet Potato Soufflé

serves 6 to 8

4 medium sweet potatoes, unpeeled
½ cup (1 stick) butter
¼ cup brown sugar, packed
2 eggs, beaten, room temperature
½ to 1 teaspoon each cinnamon, ginger, and
  freshly grated nutmeg, to taste
dash of sea salt or fresh lemon juice
½ to ¾ cup evaporated milk, heated
1 cup brown sugar, packed
¼ cup light cream
2 tablespoons butter
¾ cup pecan halves

◇ Preheat oven to 350°F.
◇ Boil sweet potatoes until tender.
◇ Peel and mash potatoes while warm.
◇ Add butter, sugar, eggs, and spices; whip until blended.
◇ Continue whipping and add enough warm milk to make a light, fluffy mixture.
◇ Spread into a greased 9-inch square casserole or a 2-quart soufflé dish.
◇ Combine sugar, cream, and butter in a saucepan over medium heat and bring to a boil; boil 2 to 3 minutes.
◇ Sprinkle pecans over sweet potatoes; pour sugar mixture over pecans.
◇ Bake 20 to 30 minutes or until glaze begins to bubble.

Vegetable Pâté

makes 2 cups

8 ounces fresh stringless green beans
1 clove garlic, finely minced
1 medium onion, finely chopped
3 tablespoons butter
10 ounces fresh mushrooms, finely minced
½ cup fresh parsley, finely minced
2 teaspoons fresh lemon juice
sea salt and freshly ground white pepper, to taste
2 hard cooked eggs, chopped
2 to 3 tablespoons mayonnaise (enough to bind
  ingredients)
cayenne pepper generously, but to taste
sour cream and fresh parsley

◇ Blanch, drain, and finely chop green beans; set aside.
◇ Sauté garlic and onion in hot butter over medium heat until soft but not browned.
◇ Add mushrooms and cook over medium heat until moisture evaporates; stir to eliminate sticking.
◇ Add green beans, parsley, lemon juice, salt, and pepper; heat until blended; cool.
◇ Add chopped eggs, mayonnaise, salt, pepper, and cayenne pepper.
◇ Check seasoning.
◇ Pour into a 2-cup mold which has been lined with plastic wrap.
◇ Cover and refrigerate overnight.
◇ Unmold and top with sour cream and minced parsley.
◇ Serve with pumpernickel rounds.

Wild Rice with Pecans

serves 8

2 cups wild rice
4 tablespoons butter
2 stalks celery, finely diced
1 medium onion, finely chopped
²/₃ cup fresh mushrooms, chopped
sea salt and freshly ground pepper, to taste
½ cup fresh parsley, finely minced
¾ cup toasted pecans, chopped

◇ Cook wild rice according to package directions, substituting chicken stock for water.
◇ Melt butter over medium heat and cook celery, onion, and mushrooms until just tender; stir occasionally.
◇ Season cooked rice and combine with sautéed vegetables.
◇ Check seasoning.
◇ Just before serving, add fresh parsley and toasted pecans; toss lightly.

Zucchini with *Kasséri* Cheese

serves 10

8 medium zucchini, about 2 pounds
2 medium onions, chopped
4 tablespoons butter
4 eggs, beaten
sea salt and freshly ground white pepper, to taste
1 cup Kasséri cheese, grated

◇ Cut zucchini into ¼-inch slices; salt; drain in colander.
◇ Butter a 7-by-11-inch glass casserole.
◇ Steam zucchini for about 8 minutes or until just tender; drain; place in casserole.
◇ Sauté onions in hot butter over medium heat until soft but not browned.
◇ Preheat oven to 375°F.
◇ Combine beaten eggs, onions, seasoning, and cheese; pour over zucchini.
◇ Check seasoning.
◇ Bake for 20 minutes or until cheese is golden and bubbly.

SALADS AND DRESSINGS

Country French Dressing

makes 1 pint

1 teaspoon dry mustard
1 teaspoon paprika
1/2 teaspoon sea salt
1/4 cup onions
3 tablespoons fresh lemon juice
3 tablespoons vinegar
1/2 cup honey
1 cup vegetable oil
1 tablespoon celery seeds
sea salt and freshly ground pepper, to taste

◇ Combine mustard, paprika, and salt in a
   bowl until blended.
◇ Blend or process onion.
◇ Add mustard mixture, lemon juice, vinegar, and honey; blend or process 1 minute.
◇ While blender or processor is running, add
   oil slowly until blended.
◇ Pour into pint jar and stir in celery seeds.
◇ Check seasoning; add salt and pepper to
   taste.
   (For best results, prepare several hours
   or a day in advance.)

Garlic Dressing

makes 1 cup

2 to 3 cloves garlic, finely minced, to taste
juice of 4 lemons
2/3 cup olive oil (about), adjust to taste
sea salt and freshly ground pepper, to taste
fresh parsley (optional), finely minced

◇ Combine all ingredients in a pint jar and
   shake well.
   (For best results, prepare 3 to 4 hours or
   a day in advance.)

German Potato Salad with Bacon Dressing

serves 12 to 15

18 medium boiling potatoes (about 6 pounds)
   scrubbed but not peeled
1 pound bacon
1 cup onions, finely chopped
1/2 cup white wine vinegar
1/4 to 1/2 cup water
sea salt and freshly ground pepper, to taste
1/4 cup fresh parsley, finely minced

◇ Drop potatoes in large pot of salted, boiling
   water and cook until a fork easily
   pierces. Do not overcook.
◇ Drain potatoes; cut into 1/4-inch slices; set
   aside in a covered bowl while the dressing is prepared.
◇ Cook bacon over moderate heat until
   brown and crisp. Drain on paper towels,
   dice, and reserve.
◇ Add onions to the bacon fat and sauté until
   soft and transparent but not browned.
◇ Add remaining ingredients and stir until
   blended.
◇ Check seasoning.
◇ Pour the hot sauce over the warm potatoes
   and toss gently until potatoes are evenly
   coated.
◇ Leave at room temperature until serving
   time.
◇ When ready to serve, add bacon bits and
   parsley; toss gently.

Molded Cranberry Apple Salad

makes 16 small servings

6-ounce package cherry gelatin
1 cup hot water
1 cup pineapple juice
16-ounce can crushed pineapple, drained
1 cup unpared apples, cored and chopped
1 cup raw cranberries, chopped
1/2 to 1 cup sugar, to taste
1 cup pecans or walnuts, chopped
sour cream

◇ Combine gelatin with hot water and stir until dissolved.
◇ Add pineapple juice and refrigerate until partially set.
◇ Combine crushed pineapple, chopped apples, and cranberries with sugar; add to partially set gelatin.
◇ Add nuts and pour into a 7- by 11-inch glass casserole.
◇ Cover with plastic wrap and refrigerate. (This can be prepared a day in advance.)
◇ Cut into serving portions and place on a bed of greens.
◇ Garnish with sour cream.

Oriental Bean Sprout Salad

serves 8

1/2 pound pea pods, fresh or frozen, with edges trimmed
1 pound bean sprouts

Dressing
1/2 cup peanut oil
1/4 cup sesame oil
2 tablespoons soy sauce
2 cloves crushed garlic
juice of 1 lemon

◇ Steam pea pods for 5 minutes. (If using frozen pea pods, cook for 3 minutes in boiling water.)
◇ Wash and drain sprouts.
◇ Combine pods and sprouts in large bowl. Prepare dressing and pour over the vegetables, tossing sprouts and pods to absorb dressing.

Tahini Dressing

makes 1 cup

4 cloves garlic, finely minced
4 tablespoons tahini
6 tablespoons olive oil
4 tablespoons fresh lemon juice
sea salt and freshly ground pepper, to taste
cayenne pepper (optional)
4 to 6 tablespoons warm water

◇ Place all ingredients, except water, in a blender or food processor and blend until smooth.
◇ Add water gradually until desired consistency is reached.
◇ Check seasoning.
◇ Serve at room temperature. (For best results, prepare 2 to 3 hours in advance.)

DESSERTS

Amaretto Ice Cream Pie

serves 6 to 8

½ gallon butter pecan ice cream, softened
¼ to ½ cup Amaretto, to taste
9-inch prepared graham cracker pie shell
½ cup pecan pieces, toasted
1 cup freshly whipped cream

◇ Quickly combine softened ice cream with
Amaretto until blended.
◇ Pour into prepared pie shell, piling the ice
cream higher in the center.
◇ Sprinkle top with toasted pecan pieces.
◇ Cover with plastic wrap and refreeze until
serving time.
◇ Cut into serving portions; pipe with freshly
whipped cream.
◇ Serve immediately.
(This may be prepared weeks in ad-
vance, covered completely, and stored in
an airtight plastic bag in freezer.)

Autumn Apple Cake

serves 12 to 15

1 cup vegetable oil
3 eggs, room temperature
2 cups sugar
1 teaspoon vanilla
2 cups flour, sifted
1 teaspoon baking soda
½ teaspoon salt
2 to 3 teaspoons cinnamon
4 cups apples, peeled and thinly sliced (Jonathan
  or Winesap)
1 cup walnuts, chopped

◇ Preheat oven to 350°F.
◇ Grease and flour a 9- by 13-inch pan.
◇ Combine oil, eggs, sugar, and vanilla; beat
until fluffy.
◇ Sift dry ingredients and add to egg mix-
ture; blend well.
◇ Fold in apples and nuts; pour into baking
pan.
◇ Bake for 45 to 50 minutes.
◇ Prepare icing.

Icing
6 ounces cream cheese, room temperature
3 tablespoons butter, room temperature
2 teaspoons vanilla
1½ cups confectioner's sugar, sifted

◇ Combine all ingredients and beat until
smooth and creamy.
◇ Spread icing on cooled cake.
(For best results, prepare cake the day
before.)

Babas *au Rhum*

16 ½-cup molds or 8 1-cup molds

Sugar Syrup
2 cups water
1 cup sugar
⅓ cup dark rum (including reserved rum from currants)

Babas
⅔ cup currants
½ cup dark rum
1 package dry yeast
¼ cup warm milk
1 teaspoon sugar
2 cups flour, unsifted
3 tablespoons sugar
½ teaspoon salt
4 eggs, room temperature
¼ cup heavy cream
12 tablespoons butter

◊ Heat sugar and water in a medium sized saucepan over low heat until sugar is dissolved.
◊ Boil 2 to 3 minutes or until syrup becomes clear.
◊ Set aside to cool.
◊ Marinate currants in rum and set aside.
◊ Combine yeast with milk and sugar and let stand 5 minutes or until frothy.
◊ Place flour, sugar, and salt in a food processor and process with 3 to 4 quick on–offs.
◊ Add eggs, cream, and yeast mixture to processor and process with on–offs until mixture is smooth.
◊ Cover the processor bowl and let dough rise in a warm place until doubled, 45 minutes to 1 hour.
◊ Add softened butter to risen dough and process until blended.

◊ Stir in drained currants.
◊ Add ⅓ cup rum to sugar syrup (including reserved rum from currants).
◊ Grease baba molds; chill and then rebutter molds.
◊ Fill molds ⅓ full; cover. Let rise in a warm place until molds are almost full, 45 minutes to 1 hour.
◊ Preheat oven to 400°F; bake babas for 10 minutes.
◊ Lower heat to 350°F and bake until they are golden brown and begin to shrink from sides, 15 to 20 minutes.
◊ Place warm babas in syrup; carefully toss them with a slotted spoon until they become glazed.
◊ Drain on wire racks.
◊ Serve warm.
    (If using a hand mixer, combine ingredients as directed; add the butter gradually with mixer on low speed; then mix on medium speed for 2 to 3 minutes or until dough is smooth and elastic.)

Baklava

12-by 17-inch pan

1 pound phyllo *pastry, thawed as package directs*
1 to 1½ pounds sweet butter, melted at low temperature and set aside.

Syrup
2 cups sugar
1 cup water
1 tablespoon fresh lemon juice
¼ cup honey (optional)

Filling
1 pound walnuts, toasted and chopped coarsely
½ cup sugar
1 teaspoon cinnamon, to taste
cloves and freshly ground nutmeg, to taste

◊ Preheat oven to 350°F.
◊ Combine sugar and water and cook over medium heat until it comes to a boil.

◇ Add lemon juice and cook over low heat for 10 to 15 minutes; stir in honey and set syrup aside. (This can be prepared the day before.)

◇ Prepare filling by blending nuts, sugar, and spices until uniform.

◇ Place thawed *phyllo* on work surface as package instructs.

◇ Brush bottom of 12- by 17-inch baking pan with melted butter.

◇ Lay one sheet of *phyllo* in pan, butter lightly, and continue layering until half the sheets have been used.

◇ Spread filling evenly over *phyllo* layers.

◇ Place remaining sheets of *phyllo* as before, buttering lightly between each one. Brush last layer also.

◇ Use a sharp knife and gently score (cutting through all layers) into square or diamond shapes.

◇ Bake for 30 minutes; lower heat to 300°F and bake 30 minutes longer or until golden brown.

◇ Remove from oven and pour cooled syrup over hot baklava.

◇ Let sit, loosely covered, until the next day to allow flavors to blend.

◇ Serve at room temperature.
(This may be prepared several weeks in advance and stored in a cool part of the house in airtight containers.)

Bessie's Easter Pie

makes 2 9-inch pies

Crust
1 1/2 teaspoons baking powder
2/3 cup sugar
3 eggs
1 1/2 tablespoons shortening
1 1/3 cups flour

◇ Cream shortening with sugar and eggs; gradually add flour and baking powder. Batter should be stiff.

◇ Roll out dough on floured surface; roll out to end of each 9-inch pie plate. Save remaining dough.

Filling
3-pound container ricotta cheese
1 cup sugar
8 eggs
3 tablespoons orange rind
1 tablespoon lemon rind
dash cinnamon
1/2 cup semisweet chocolate chips

◇ Preheat oven to 350°F.

◇ Beat ricotta and sugar together.

◇ Add eggs, one at a time.

◇ Stir in rinds, cinnamon, and chocolate chips. Blend well.

◇ Pour filling into pie shells.

◇ With remaining dough, make 12 1/2-inch strips. On each pie, place three strips horizontally over filling and three vertically over those strips.

◇ Bake until filling is firm and crust is golden.

◇ Cool thoroughly before serving. Sprinkle with powdered sugar, if desired.

Boston Cream Pie

2 8-inch cakes

génoise *(see page 200), baked and cooled*
sugar syrup (recipe below)
vanilla cream filling (recipe below)
chocolate buttercream (recipe below)

Sugar Syrup
2 cups sugar
1 cup water

Vanilla Cream Filling
4¾-ounce package vanilla pie filling
2½ cups milk
3 tablespoons sugar
2 teaspoons vanilla
(heavy cream, as needed, to thin filling)

Chocolate Buttercream
4 to 5 ounces unsweetened chocolate, melted in a
*   double boiler and set aside*
5 egg yolks, room temperature
pinch of salt
1 to 1¼ cups confectioner's sugar, sifted
1 cup (2 sticks) butter, room temperature

◇ Bring sugar and water to a boil over medium heat.
◇ Boil 2 to 3 minutes or until clear. Let syrup cool. (This can be made in advance and stored covered in the refrigerator for several weeks.)
◇ Prepare vanilla pie filling as package directs, using only 2½ cups milk (instead of 3 cups).
◇ After filling has completely cooled, add the sugar and vanilla. (This may be prepared a day in advance and stored covered in the refrigerator.)
◇ Combine egg yolks, salt, and sugar in a separate bowl and beat with an electric mixer on high speed until mixture thickens and becomes pale yellow.
◇ Add ½ the butter and beat well.
◇ Add the chocolate and the remaining butter, one tablespoon at a time.
◇ Use immediately.

◇ Assemble Boston cream pie by taking a long serrated knife and gently splitting the cake in half horizontally.
◇ Spoon or brush sugar syrup over the cut surfaces.
◇ Place bottom half onto prepared cake plate.
◇ Spread cream filling evenly over bottom layer.
◇ Place remaining cake half on top of filling.
◇ Smooth a thick layer of chocolate buttercream over the top layer.
◇ Serve at room temperature.

Chocolate Chip Pecan Pie

1 9-inch pie

2 eggs, beaten, room temperature
1 cup sugar
½ cup all-purpose flour
½ cup (1 stick) unsalted butter, melted and cooled
1 cup chocolate chips
1 cup pecans, chopped
1 teaspoon vanilla
9 inch unbaked pie shell
whipped cream (optional)

◇ Preheat oven to 350°F.
◇ Beat eggs at high speed until light and lemon colored.
◇ Add sugar gradually.
◇ Reduce speed of mixer to low and add flour and melted butter; mix until blended.
◇ Stir in chips, nuts, and vanilla.
◇ Bake until golden brown, about 40 minutes.
◇ Serve warm. (Pass whipped cream.)

Chocolate Rum Pie

serves 6 to 8

½ cup (1 stick) unsalted butter, room temperature
⅔ cup sugar
2 ounces semisweet chocolate, melted and cooled
2 whole eggs, room temperature
2 to 3 tablespoons rum, to taste
9-inch pastry shell (see page 205), baked and
  cooled
1 cup heavy cream, whipped and sweetened

◇ Combine butter and sugar; beat until thoroughly blended and creamy.
◇ Stir in chocolate.
◇ Add eggs, one at a time, and beat for 5 minutes after each addition.
◇ Add rum and stir.
◇ Pour into baked pie shell; chill 2 hours.
◇ Before serving, spread sweetened whipped cream over top.
◇ Serve chilled.
   (This pie should be prepared the day it is to be served.)

Coeur à la Crème with Raspberries

serves 8

2 cups heavy cream, chilled
4 egg whites, room temperature
4 tablespoons heavy cream
2 8-ounce packages cream cheese, room temperature
1⅓ cups confectioner's sugar
2 teaspoons vanilla
1 quart fresh raspberries with sugar, to taste
confectioner's sugar, optional

◇ Prepare a special *coeur à la crème* mold (with perforated bottom) by lining it with 3 layers of dampened cheese cloth.
◇ Whip heavy cream; set aside.
◇ Beat egg whites until they are stiff and form soft peaks.
◇ Combine cream, cream cheese, confectioner's sugar, and vanilla; beat until light and fluffy.
◇ Stir 4 tablespoons of egg white into the cream cheese mixture.
◇ Fold remaining egg whites and whipped cream into the mixture.
◇ Pour mixture into mold and cover.
◇ Store filled mold on a rack or plate in the refrigerator overnight to allow excess liquid to drain.
◇ To serve, unmold onto chilled serving plate and remove cheese cloth.
◇ Sprinkle top with confectioner's sugar (optional).
◇ Surround with sugared raspberries.

Crème de Cassis Parfaits

serves 6

¾ cup crème de cassis
¼ cup strawberry brandy or liqueur
½ cup sliced almonds
1 cup heavy cream, whipped (reserve ¼ cup for
  topping)
1 quart natural vanilla ice cream, softened
1 pint fresh raspberries

◇ Combine ¼ cup cassis with brandy and set aside.
◇ Toast almonds until golden brown; set aside.
◇ Whip cream; set aside.
◇ Combine softened ice cream with remaining ½ cup cassis.
◇ Assemble parfaits by dividing ingredients evenly among 6 parfait glasses; make 2 layers of ice cream, whipped cream, and raspberries. (Ice cream melts quickly when combined with brandy, so work quickly, or rechill mixture and assemble once it is firm again.)
◇ Top with whipped cream, sprinkle with toasted almonds, and drizzle cassis-brandy mixture over top.
◇ Serve immediately.
   (Can be prepared ahead, covered, and stored in freezer.)

Crispy Meringue Shells

makes 12 medium shells

4 large egg whites, room temperature
dash of salt
¼ teaspoon cream of tartar
1 cup superfine sugar
1 teaspoon vanilla

◇ Prepare a 12- by 18-inch baking sheet by lining it with brown wrapping paper or parchment paper.
◇ Preheat oven to 275°F.
◇ Beat egg whites on low speed with an electric mixer until they become frothy or foamy.
◇ Add salt and cream of tartar and continue beating at high speed until soft peaks form.
◇ Add sugar gradually and continue beating on high speed until glossy, stiff peaks are formed and the sugar is dissolved. (Don't overwork or it will become watery once more.)
◇ Add vanilla; blend.
◇ Place heaping spoonfuls of meringue (divide equally into 12 portions) on the brown paper and swirl into small shells (about 3 inches wide).
◇ Bake 1½ hours, or until firm and crisp.
◇ Remove meringues with a spatula and let cool completely on cooling rack. (These may be prepared several days in advance if stored in an airtight container.)
◇ Serve at room temperature. (If you wish to double the recipe, it works better if you prepare two separate batches.)

Down's Nesselrode Pudding

serves 8 to 10

5 eggs, separated, room temperature
½ cup sugar
2 cups scalded milk
2 envelopes unflavored gelatin
1 cup light cream, cold
1 tablespoon Cognac
2 teaspoons vanilla
¼ pound macaroons, crumbled
½ cup toasted almonds, chopped
¼ cup white raisins
¾ cup mixed diced fruit and peels
½ teaspoon salt
2 tablespoons sugar
fresh whipped cream

◇ Place egg yolks in double boiler and whisk over medium heat until pale yellow.
◇ Gradually stir in the sugar and milk and cook on low heat until custard coats the spoon; stir constantly.
◇ Sprinkle gelatin over cold cream and set aside for 3 to 4 minutes or until spongy.
◇ Add softened gelatin to custard mixture and stir until completely dissolved.
◇ Remove from heat; add Cognac and vanilla.
◇ Place in refrigerator and chill until it begins to set. (Stir occasionally to determine readiness.)
◇ Fold in macaroons, almonds, raisins, and fruit.
◇ Add salt to egg whites and beat until foamy. Add sugar gradually and beat until stiff peaks are formed.
◇ Fold egg whites into chilled custard mixture.
◇ Pour into a 6 cup mold or compote.
◇ Chill 4 to 6 hours.
◇ Unmold onto a chilled serving platter and garnish with whipped cream. (This can be unmolded and refrigerated until serving time. Do not freeze.)

Fresh Strawberry Tarts

serves 18

*1 recipe vanilla cream filling, cooked and cooled
  (see page 198)*
1 egg yolk, slightly beaten
1 teaspoon water
*1 package (2 sheets) prepared puff pastry, cooked
  as directed and cooled*
½ cup currant jelly
1½ cups fresh strawberries, hulled and patted dry

◊ Preheat oven to 350°F.
◊ Whisk together the egg yolk and water and
   brush over the unbaked pastry dough.
   Take care not to drip mixture down the
   sides; it will cause the pastry to stick to
   the pan.
◊ Bake pastries as directed; cool on wire
   racks.
◊ Transfer cooled pastries to serving trays or
   plates; spread the cooled vanilla cream
   over the top of the pastry.
◊ Heat currant jelly on low heat until melted.
◊ Arrange berries over the vanilla cream
   layer.
◊ Gently brush jelly glaze over berry tops and
   around the edges of pastry.
   (This dessert is best if served within an
   hour of preparation.)

Gateau au Chocolat

serves 8

4 ounces semisweet chocolate
2 tablespoons Grand Marnier
½ cup (1 stick) butter, room temperature
⅔ cup granulated sugar
3 eggs, separated, room temperature
dash of salt
⅓ cup toasted pecans and almonds, finely ground
1 teaspoon vanilla
¾ cup cake flour, sifted

Chocolate Icing
3 ounces bittersweet chocolate
1 tablespoon strong coffee
5 tablespoons cold butter

◊ Preheat oven to 350°F.
◊ Grease and flour the sides of an 8-inch *génoise* pan.
◊ Line bottom of cake pan with a circle of
   waxed paper or parchment paper.
◊ Heat chocolate and Grand Marnier in a
   double boiler over low heat until melted;
   set aside.
◊ Cream butter and sugar (reserve 1 tablespoon of sugar) until pale yellow and
   creamy.
◊ Add egg yolks and beat until well blended.
◊ Beat egg whites with salt until soft peaks
   are formed. Add the reserved tablespoon
   sugar; beat until stiff peaks are formed.
◊ Add chocolate mixture, nuts, and vanilla to
   butter mixture and stir.
◊ Gently stir ⅓ of the egg white mixture into
   the chocolate mixture.
◊ Fold an additional ⅓ of egg whites into
   batter.
◊ Gently alternate folding remaining egg
   whites and flour until both are incorporated.
◊ Spoon batter into pan and bake for 25 to 30
   minutes. (Cake should remain underdone; it will rise, form a crust on the
   top, but the center will remain wobbly
   when shaken.)

◇ Allow to cool in pan for 10 minutes.
◇ Run a metal spatula around edge and gently invert onto cooling rack.
◇ Let cool 1 to 2 hours or overnight.
   (Cake may be prepared a day in advance, cooled, and wrapped tightly in aluminum foil and iced the next day.)
◇ Prepare chocolate icing by heating chocolate and coffee in a double boiler on low heat until melted.
◇ Remove chocolate mixture from heat and immediately begin whisking in the cold butter, one tablespoon at a time.
   (Icing will become firm as it cools.)
◇ Whisk until icing is of spreading consistency.
◇ Spread over cooled cake.

Génoise with Apricot Glaze

makes 2 8-inch *génoise*

4 large eggs (¾ cup), room temperature
dash of salt
⅔ cup sugar
¾ cup cake flour, sifted
4 tablespoons unsalted butter, melted and set aside
1 teaspoon vanilla

Apricot Glaze
1 cup apricot preserves or jam
2 tablespoons Kirsch (optional)

◇ Prepare *génoise* pans by brushing melted butter evenly around side of pans and dusting sides lightly with flour.
◇ Line bottoms of pans with a circle of waxed paper.
◇ Preheat oven to 350°F.
◇ Break eggs into a double boiler or in a large copper bowl over a pan of hot water. (Water in double boiler must not boil nor touch the bottom of the bowl.)
◇ Place pan over low heat and begin beating eggs.
◇ Add salt and gradually begin adding sugar, beating with an electric mixer on high speed for 4 to 5 minutes or until mixture thickens, increases in volume, and forms a thick, pale yellow ribbon. Batter will be warm.
◇ Remove egg mixture from heat, add vanilla, reduce mixer to low speed, and continue beating until the mixture is cool, 3 to 4 minutes.
◇ Quickly and gently fold the flour into the egg mixture in 3 batches.
◇ Quickly fold in the butter with the last batch of flour.
◇ Pour immediately and gently into prepared pans.
◇ Bake for 30 to 35 minutes or until the cake shrinks slightly from sides of pan.
◇ Cool 10 minutes in the pan, and then invert onto a cooling rack. (The cake will drop out of the pan.)
◇ Remove waxed paper.
◇ Let cool at least 1 hour.
◇ Prepare glaze by heating jam and kirsch over low heat until melted.
◇ Strain through a fine meshed strainer.
◇ Brush melted warm glaze over cooled *génoise*.

Variation
Lemon *Génoise*: Substitute the grated rind of 1 lemon for vanilla flavoring.

Giant Granola Cookies

approximately 1 dozen

½ cup soft shortening
1 cup brown sugar, firmly packed
1 egg
3 tablespoons milk
1 teaspoon vanilla
1¼ cups flour, sifted
½ teaspoon soda
dash of salt
2 cups natural granola cereal (no preservatives)

◇ Preheat oven to 350°F.
◇ Combine shortening, sugar, egg, milk, and
   vanilla, beat until creamy.
◇ Combine dry ingredients and add to
   creamed mixture; blend well.
◇ Stir in granola cereal.
◇ Scoop with ice cream scooper onto greased
   baking sheets.
◇ Use a spatula or glass dipped in sugar and
   flatten dough to ¼ inch thick.
◇ Bake 10 minutes.
◇ Let cool for 1 to 2 minutes; then remove to
   cooling racks.

Ginger Cream

serves 2 to 4

2 tablespoons confectioner's sugar
1 pint heavy cream, whipped
½ teaspoon powdered ginger
2 tablespoons crystallized ginger, very finely diced

◇ Beat sugar into whipped cream.
◇ Fold gingers into cream.
◇ Store covered in refrigerator.
◇ Serve chilled.
   (This may be prepared 1 to 2 hours in
   advance.)

Holiday Pumpkin Roll

serves 10 to 12

3 eggs, beaten, room temperature
1 cup sugar
⅔ cup canned pumpkin
1 teaspoon fresh lemon juice
¾ cup flour, sifted
1 teaspoon baking powder
½ teaspoon salt
2 tablespoons ground cinnamon
1 teaspoon ground ginger
½ teaspoon nutmeg, freshly grated
1 cup walnuts, coarsely chopped
confectioner's sugar

Filling
12 ounces cream cheese
4 tablespoons butter, room temperature
1 cup confectioner's sugar
1 teaspoon vanilla

◇ Grease and flour the sides of a 10- by 15-
   by 1-inch jelly roll pan. Line the bottom
   of pan with waxed paper.
◇ Preheat oven to 375°F.
◇ Combine eggs and sugar and beat until
   light colored and frothy, about 3 to 4
   minutes.
◇ Mix in pumpkin and lemon juice.
◇ Combine flour, baking powder, salt, cinnamon, ginger, and nutmeg; fold into
   pumpkin mixture.
◇ Pour into baking pan; sprinkle top with
   nuts.
◇ Bake 12 to 15 minutes or until top springs
   back when touched. (Cooks quickly;
   don't overcook.)
◇ Sift confectioner's sugar onto a clean dish
   towel.
◇ Remove cake from oven and invert onto
   towel.
◇ Remove waxed paper.
◇ While cake is very warm, roll cake and
   towel together (as in a jelly roll).
◇ Set aside to cool for about an hour, seam
   side down.

◇ Blend cream cheese and butter until light and fluffy.
◇ Gradually add sugar and vanilla; beat until smooth.
◇ Unroll cake after cooling and spread filling, leaving a ½-inch edge on all sides.
◇ Reroll, cover, and refrigerate.
(This can be prepared a day in advance.)

Homemade Blueberry Tarts

makes 8 3½-inch tarts

8 3½-inch prepared graham cracker tart crusts
cream cheese filling (recipe below)
blueberry filling (recipe below)
natural vanilla ice cream

Cream Cheese Filling
8-ounce package cream cheese, room temperature
⅓ cup plus 1 tablespoon sugar
1 egg, room temperature
2 teaspoons fresh lemon juice
1 teaspoon vanilla

Blueberry Filling
1 can blueberries, drained (reserve juice)
¼ cup flour
½ cup sugar
¾ cup blueberry juice
2 to 3 tablespoons fresh lemon juice
dash of salt

◇ Preheat oven to 350°F.
◇ Prepare cream cheese filling by combining all ingredients and beating until smooth and creamy.
◇ Divide equally into 8 unbaked tart crusts and bake for 15 to 20 minutes or until crusts are golden brown.
◇ Cool; set aside until serving time.
◇ Prepare blueberry filling by placing flour and sugar in saucepan and mixing until uniformly blended.
◇ Add reserved juice and cook over medium heat until sauce is of medium thickness; stir constantly.

◇ Remove from heat; add lemon juice, salt, and blueberries.
◇ Cool; chill until serving time.
◇ To serve, place 1 tablespoon blueberry filling onto each tart and top with a spoonful of vanilla ice cream.

Ice Cream Delight Birthday Cake

serves 6 to 8

1 quart mint chocolate chip natural ice cream, softened
1 quart lemon custard natural ice cream, softened
1 quart strawberry natural ice cream, softened
1 quart butter pecan natural ice cream, softened
1 quart chocolate fudge natural ice cream, softened
fresh flowers, leaves, candied violets, toasted nuts, or shaved chocolate, for garnish

◇ Chill a 5- by 9-inch metal mold or baking pan in the refrigerator or freezer.
◇ Spread a ½-inch layer of each variety ice cream (one on top of the other) in the mold. (If ice cream becomes too soft to spread, place in freezer and allow to become solid again.)
◇ Cover mold and return to freezer for at least 6 hours.
◇ To unmold, remove cover and place a serving platter on top; invert the mold and the platter.
◇ Wipe outside of mold several times with a towel wrung out in hot water; lift mold. (Ice Cream cake can be unmolded ahead and returned to the freezer until serving time.)
◇ Garnish and slice.
◇ Serve immediately.

Lemon Bars

30 bars

½ cup confectioner's sugar
2¼ cups flour
1 cup butter (2 sticks), room temperature
4 eggs, beaten
2 cups granulated sugar
⅓ cup fresh lemon juice
¼ cup flour
½ teaspoon baking powder
confectioner's sugar

◇ Preheat oven to 350°F.
◇ Mix sugar and 2 cups flour until uniform.
◇ Add butter and blend until the mixture clings together.
◇ Press butter mixture evenly over bottom of a 9- by 13-inch baking pan.
◇ Bake 20 to 25 minutes, or until lightly browned.
◇ Combine eggs, sugar, and lemon juice.
◇ Add ¼ cup flour and baking powder; mix just until dry ingredients are blended.
◇ Pour lemon mixture over baked crust and continue baking an additional 25 minutes.
◇ Remove from oven.
◇ Dust with confectioner's sugar; cool.
◇ Cut into squares.

Lemon Chess Tarts

makes 24 3-inch tarts or 1 9-inch pie shell

Tart or Pastry Dough
2⅔ cups flour, sifted
1 teaspoon salt
1 cup (2 sticks) butter, cut into 1-inch pieces, room temperature
2 egg yolks, room temperature
2 tablespoons sugar (for sweet desserts only)
4 tablespoons ice water

Chess Filling
3 eggs, room temperature
1½ cups sugar
juice of 1½ lemons
zest of 1 lemon
dash of salt
3 tablespoons unsalted butter, melted and cooled
1 tablespoon yellow corn meal

◇ Place flour and salt in mixing bowl.
◇ Make a well in center of the flour and place butter, egg yolks, and sugar in the well.
◇ Use fingertips and rub or gently pinch flour and butter together until it becomes a uniform mixture; it will become coarse and mealy.
◇ Add water, one tablespoon at a time, and toss mixture lightly with a fork or with fingertips until it begins to hold together.
◇ Form dough into a ball; wrap in plastic wrap and chill for at least 30 minutes. (This can be prepared 2 to 3 days in advance.)
◇ Lightly grease pans.
◇ Roll out chilled dough and line pans; rechill.
◇ Preheat oven to 350°F.
◇ Combine eggs and sugar and beat with an electric mixer on low speed until well blended.
◇ Add remaining filling ingredients and mix.
◇ Place chilled pans on a baking sheet and fill ¾ full.
◇ Bake 20 to 25 minutes or until golden.
◇ Remove from oven and place on cooling rack, 5 to 10 minutes.
◇ Unmold tarts and continue cooling.
◇ Serve warm or at room temperature.

Linzer Cookies

makes 4 dozen

1½ cups (3 sticks) butter, room temperature
1 cup sugar
2 egg yolks, room temperature
1 teaspoon vanilla
4 cups flour, sifted
12-ounce jar raspberry preserves

◇ Cream butter and sugar until light and fluffy.
◇ Add egg yolks and vanilla; blend.
◇ Add flour; mix until all ingredients are combined (batter will be stiff).
◇ Preheat oven to 350°F.
◇ Shape dough into balls the size of a small walnut.
◇ Place dough on ungreased baking sheets.
◇ Make a thumb imprint in the top of each ball and fill indentation with ½ teaspoon preserves.
◇ Bake 15 to 20 minutes or until golden.
◇ Let cool on wire racks.
  (These may be prepared 2 to 3 days in advance and stored in airtight container.)

Mexican Wedding Cookies

makes 3 dozen

1 cup (2 sticks) unsalted butter, room temperature
½ cup confectioner's sugar, sifted
2 cups flour, sifted
pinch of salt
1 cup toasted pecans, chopped finely
1 teaspoon vanilla
confectioner's sugar

◇ Preheat oven to 350°F.
◇ Grease baking sheet and set aside.
◇ Cream butter until light and fluffy.
◇ Add sugar, flour, salt, pecans, and vanilla; mix until well blended.
◇ Form dough into balls the size of a large walnut or into half moon shapes.
◇ Place cookies about 2 inches apart on baking sheet; bake 15 to 20 minutes or until pale golden (they should not brown).
◇ Transfer cookies to wire rack to cool.
◇ Sift or dust confectioner's sugar over cookies while still warm.
◇ Cool.
  (These may be made in advance and stored in airtight containers.)

Orange Rum Raisin Bombe

serves 6

1 quart orange ice or sherbet, softened
1½ quarts rum raisin ice cream, softened
½ cup cognac or rum

◇ Chill a 2-quart ice cream or other mold in the freezer.
◇ Spread the inside of the mold with orange ice. (Layer should be about ½ inch thick.)
◇ Press the ice against the mold with the back of a spoon or spatula to insure it takes the shape of the mold.
◇ Place mold in freezer for 5 minutes to re-set.
◇ Pack the ice cream into the center of the mold.
◇ Cover mold with mold lid or with foil.
◇ Freeze for at least 6 hours.
◇ To unmold, remove lid or foil and place a serving plate on top; invert the mold and plate together.
◇ Wipe outside of mold several times with a towel wrung out in hot water; lift mold. (Bombe can be unmolded ahead and returned to the freezer until serving time.)
◇ Slice bombe; top each serving with a spoonful of cognac or rum.
◇ Serve immediately.

Poached Pears

serves 2 to 4

1 cup sugar
2 cups water
zest of 1 lemon
2 to 4 fresh pears (Anjou or Bosc)
juice of 1 lemon
1 teaspoon vanilla

◇ Select a saucepan that will hold the (whole) pears when standing upright.
◇ Bring sugar and water to a boil; reduce heat to medium and add lemon zest; simmer 5 to 10 minutes.
◇ Peel pears (leave the stems) and very carefully remove core from the bottom of the pear.
◇ Sprinkle pears generously with lemon juice as soon as they are peeled.
◇ Cut a thin slice from the bottom of pears (to allow them to stand upright).
◇ Immerse pears in syrup and gently simmer for 5 to 10 minutes, turning and basting with syrup until fork tender. Cooking time will vary depending on the ripeness and quality of the pears.
◇ Remove from heat; cool pears in syrup.
◇ Drain pears; cover; and chill in refrigerator.
◇ Serve with ginger cream.

Uncle Sam's Chocolate Cake

serves 16 to 30

½ cup (1 stick) butter
1 cup sugar
4 eggs, room temperature
16 ounces hot fudge sauce
1 cup flour, sifted

◇ Preheat oven to 350°F.
◇ Grease and flour a 9- by 13-inch baking pan.
◇ Combine butter, sugar, and eggs; beat until light and creamy.
◇ Add hot fudge sauce and flour; beat until combined thoroughly.
◇ Pour into greased and floured pan.
◇ Bake for about 35 minutes.
◇ Prepare frosting.

Frosting
6 tablespoons butter
1½ cups sugar
8 tablespoons heavy cream
½ cup chocolate chips
½ cup walnuts, chopped (optional)

◇ Combine butter, sugar, and cream in a saucepan and bring to a boil over medium heat for about 1 minute; stir occasionally.
◇ Remove from heat and add chocolate chips; stir until blended.
◇ Spread frosting on warm cake.
◇ Sprinkle top with walnuts (optional).
   (For best results, allow cake to sit one day before cutting. This can be prepared a day or two in advance.)

Warm Apple Raisin Pie

serves 6 to 8

2 recipes pastry dough, unbaked (see page 203), or
   2 prepared 9-inch deep-dish pie shells, thawed
1 egg white, slightly beaten
7 cups Winesap apples (6 to 8 medium), pared, cored, and thinly sliced
2 to 4 tablespoons fresh lemon juice
½ cup raisins
¼ cup rum
6 to 8 tablespoons butter, cut into 1-inch pieces
¾ cup brown sugar, packed
¼ cup flour
3 teaspoons cinnamon
½ teaspoon nutmeg, freshly grated

◇ Preheat oven to 425°F.
◇ Brush bottom of pastry with beaten egg; set aside.
◇ Prepare apples and combine with lemon juice, raisins, rum, and butter; set aside.
◇ Blend sugar, flour, and cinnamon and add to apple-raisin mixture; toss until evenly coated; pour into glazed pastry shell.
◇ Brush edge of bottom pastry with egg glaze.
◇ Place top pastry over filling; seal edges.
◇ Brush top pastry with egg glaze; prick or vent pastry several times with fork.
◇ Bake 50 minutes. (If top pastry darkens too quickly, cover with aluminum foil and finish baking.)
◇ Serve warm.

BEVERAGES

Café Mexicano

makes 12 large mugs

8 to 9 ounces semisweet chocolate, to taste
1½ quarts milk (6 cups)
⅓ cup sugar
2 teaspoons almond extract, to taste
1½ teaspoons cinnamon, to taste
6 cups strong hot coffee
1½ cups brandy (about 2 tablespoons per mug)
cinnamon sticks (optional)

◇ Combine chocolate and milk over low heat and cook until chocolate melts; stir constantly.
◇ Transfer milk and melted chocolate to a blender or processor.
◇ Add sugar, almond extract, and cinnamon to milk mixture and blend about 30 seconds.
◇ Fill mugs half full with milk mixture.
◇ Add enough hot coffee to almost fill the mugs.
◇ Add brandy to each mug and garnish with cinnamon sticks.

Champagne Punch

serves 15 to 20

1 cup fresh lemon juice
1 cup superfine sugar
1½ quarts pineapple juice
1 quart fresh orange juice
1 prepared ice ring, of choice
1 fifth sauterne
2 fifths champagne

◇ Heat lemon juice and sugar until sugar is dissolved; let cool.
◇ Combine sugar-lemon mixture with other juices; cover and chill.
◇ At serving time, pour juice mixture over ice ring in punch bowl.
◇ Add wines; stir.
◇ Serve chilled.

Cinnamon Coffee

1 serving

hot coffee
1 teaspoon sugar
1 teaspoon instant chocolate mix
dash of nutmeg, freshly grated
1 cinnamon stick
heavy or light cream, optional

◇ Place sugar, chocolate mix, and nutmeg in heated coffee mug.
◇ Fill mug with hot coffee and stir with cinnamon stick.
◇ Add cream.
◇ Serve hot.

Fish House Punch

makes 5 quarts

1 quart ice mold of strong green tea (9 teaspoons of tea per quart of water)
3 cups fresh lemon juice
zest of 5 lemons
1 cup superfine sugar
1 fifth dark rum
1 fifth golden rum
1 fifth brandy or bourbon
1 bottle dry white wine
1 cup peach brandy (optional)

◇ Prepare green tea ice mold and freeze.
◇ Heat lemon juice, zest, and sugar over medium heat until sugar is dissolved.
◇ Add remaining ingredients, except frozen tea; let sit at room temperature for 2 to 3 hours. (This can be prepared a day in advance.)
◇ At serving time, place green tea ice mold in punch bowl and add rum mixture; stir.
◇ Serve chilled.

RECIPE INDEX

DESSERTS

BEVERAGES

ABOUT THE AUTHORS

Marjorie Reed is one of America's most celebrated hostesses. She has been cited in *The Bloomingdale's Book of Entertaining* and is the author of *Marjorie Reed's Party Book*. Ms. Reed was recently named the Lifestyle Advocate for Spiegel, one of the largest mail-order companies in the country, serving as a general consultant to their catalog. She makes her home in New York City.

Kalia Lulow is the co-author of nine nonfiction titles, including *Marjorie Reed's Party Book* and *Helena Rubenstein's Book of the Sun*, for which she was also the associate editor and illustrator. Ms. Lulow also writes for ABC TV Children's Programming and lives in New York City.

◇────────────────◇

ABOUT THE FOOD EDITOR

Marilyn Kelly is a gourmet cooking instructor and lecturer in her home town of Huntington, West Virginia, and throughout the Southeast. She has studied at Lavarenne Ecole de Cuisine and Academie du Vin in Paris. Ms. Kelly served as Food Consultant on *Marjorie Reed's Party Book*.

ABOUT THE ILLUSTRATOR

Robert Penny's illustrations and designs have appeared in the Potpourri Press Cookbook series, *Fancy Folds, Double Duty Decorating, For the Love of Food,* and *Marjorie Reed's Party Book.* He is a regular contributor to *Good Housekeeping, and Seventeen.* Mr. Penny lives and works in New York.

Color Photo Credits

Spring or Summer Wedding Tea
Cile Belle Fleur Burbridge: wedding cake; Hinson & Co.: fabric for tablecloth.
Special Thank You to: Harry Hinson

Thanksgiving Feast
Buccellati, Inc.: silver flatware, silver goblets, silver salt and pepper dishes; James II Gallery: dinner plates, silver napkin holders; Leron, Inc.: placemats, napkins; Mitsukoshi U.S.A., Inc.: bowl for topiary tree; Mrs. Carleton Varney: column relief centerpiece.
Special Thank You to: Mrs. Edward Munves, Sr.; Mr. Luca Buccellati, Mrs. Joanna Carson

Superbowl Sunday Fiesta
Mrs. Dasha Epstein: pepper wreath; Pan American Phoenix: glass vitrine, candlestick, terra-cotta and clay serving dishes, margarita glasses, tin dinner plates, baskets; Putumayo Gallery: serape tablecloth, handmade carousel.
Special Thank You to: Mrs. Martha Bartos, Cynthia Mead

The First and Finest Anniversary
Michaele Volbrach for Burlington Industries: bed sheets, comforter, and pillows; Mitsukoshi U.S.A. Inc.: red parasol, red lacquer vases, black lacquer tray; Pot Covers: wisteria vine basket.
Special Thank You to: Elaine Morikawa

Have a Heart Valentine's Day Dessert Party
James II Gallery: gold pedestal dish, chest of drawers; David Webb: gold cage; Spiegel Catalog: cake plates.
Special Thank You to: Mrs. Edward Munves, Sr., Mrs. Dorothy Smith

Mother's Day Brunch
Mayhew: hand-painted glasses and plates, butter and jam plates, vases, tea pot, creamer and sugar dish; Newel Art Galleries: Art Deco tea cart.
Special Thank You to: Bruce Newman, Roderick Kennedy, Jr.

Sparklers and Stripes Forever Fourth of July Barbecue
Henri Bendel, Inc.: napkins, flag fans; Spiegel Catalog: wicker tables, flatware.
Special Thank You to: Nina Santisi

Greek Holiday Buffet
Kosho Ltd.: votive candle holders; Niedermaier Design: columns and capitals, Greek head and bust; Tiffany & Co.: Imari dinner plates, crystal decanters, crystal bowl, crystal platter, crystal oval dish, crystal candlesticks.
Special Thank You to: Charlene Drawheim, Carol Powers Gordon, Gene Marconi

Cover
Buccellati: silver flatware; James II Gallery: shell plates; Arnold Scaasi: Marjorie Reed's dress; Tiffany & Co.: crystal stemware, crystal shell, crystal vases, wine decanter.
Special Thank You to: Mrs. Edward Munves, Sr., Charlene Drawheim, Mr. Luca Buccellati